NAVIGATING

RELIGIOUS

DIVERSITY

IN THE GLOBAL BUSINESS
ENVIRONMENT

A PRACTICAL APPROACH

Samuel L. Dunn PhD, DBA, MBA

Joshua D. Jensen EdD, MBA, MPA

Ronald R. Galloway PhD, MS, MA

ISBN EBOOK: 978-1-7333039-0-3
ISBN PAPERBACK: 978-1-7333039-1-0
ISBN AUDIOBOOK: 978-1-7333039-2-7

Cover design by Michael J. Jensen

Printed in the USA

TABLE OF CONTENTS

This page intentionally left blank

FOREWORD

We live in a world today of increasing division, a lack of cross-cultural understanding, and a growing trend toward nationalistic attitudes. Much of this can be connected to a sense of conflict and competition between religious ideologies and beliefs.

In 1994, while serving as Minister of Education of the Republic of Kazakhstan, I initiated the creation of the Kazakh-American Free University, the first private university in Kazakhstan founded around the concept of international partnership. Some of my original goals for this university included teaching and studying in English, learning the Western free-market business system, and pursuing an international education through significant cross-cultural exchanges and internships with American students and teachers. At the time, as our newly independent country was still emerging from its past as part of the Soviet Union, this was seen as something quite radical and even risky.

The first American partner of this university was InterVarsity, an American Christian student organization. Many people were against this, claiming that this group was all about "promoting religion." However, I saw something different in the Americans that I met at that time. I saw the potential to work together in the pursuit of mutually beneficial goals in a spirit of mutual respect and cultural understanding.

Today, our university is celebrating its 25th year and it is recognized as one of the top 5 of humanities/economic universities in Kazakhstan. The university has over 4,000 students and it offers

Bachelor's, Master's and Ph.D. degrees through four academic departments: Pedagogy and Psychology, Foreign Languages, Business, and Law and International Relations. The university also has two vocational colleges. The university has distinguished itself with its focus on leadership development and numerous mutually beneficial international partnerships and programs. The university hosts 20 to 30 volunteer visiting teachers each year and over 700 students have participated in some form of international exchange or education programs.

All of this has been made possible because people from different cultures, religions and backgrounds decided to work together in a spirit of understanding toward mutually beneficial goals. In many ways, our university reflects the policies of our country's government and Kazakhstan's first president, Nursultan Nazarbayev. Kazakhstan is a multi-ethnic country with a diverse population representing numerous religions, languages and cultures. These include, as an example, Kazakhs, Russians, Ukrainians, Uzbeks, Germans, Tatars, Uyghurs, and Koreans, to name just a few. Nursultan Nazarbayev helped to build Kazakhstan around principles of tolerance and a multi-ethnic society that would live and work peacefully together. Today, Kazakhstan is one of the most stable and peaceful countries in Central Asia.

Very early in our university's development, we began a partnership with Northwest Nazarene University (NNU) in Nampa, Idaho. At that time, we became acquainted with two of the authors of this book, Dr. Samuel Dunn and Dr. Ron Galloway. These gentlemen, along with a number of other NNU professors, visited our university regularly. In addition to teaching at our university, they demonstrated a unique desire to build programs with us that would be beneficial to both of our universities. As a result, our university was able to embark on many "firsts." We sent our first student abroad to receive a double-degree in partnership with NNU. We sent our first students abroad to receive Master's degrees in partnership with NNU. And, Dr. Galloway played a key role in coaching us and helping us to receive our first international business program accreditation through the Accreditation Council for Business Schools and Programs (ACBSP) in the USA.

Dr. Dunn and Dr. Galloway talked openly about their beliefs as Christians and we knew that their university, Northwest Nazarene University, was a Christian university. But, we experienced a special level of openness, acceptance and sensitivity from them. Their desire, through our partnership, was not to "teach us," but instead, to learn together with us. We also experienced this same attitude and atmosphere at NNU. NNU welcomed and accepted our students and their university was open to students from any belief or religion. Again, their desire at NNU was to learn together with our students. They believed that by bringing together our many backgrounds and cultures, we could learn from each other and be the better for it. I am very pleased about this book and the desire of the authors to help people from different cultures and religions work together in business.

This book describes the important mechanisms necessary for building meaningful relationships, independent of religious backgrounds. Those that do this will be an important example for the young people of our world, helping them to become people who walk on the right path, living with understanding and acceptance of others. I see this as a truly holy and blessed endeavour in today's world of division and misunderstanding. I know you, the reader, will find the wisdom and advice found in this book to be insightful and helpful as you continue the work of the authors to build mutually beneficial endeavours around the world.

Yerezhep A. Mambetkaziyev, Doctor of Chemistry
President, Kazakh-American Free University
Oskemen, Kazakhstan
Former Minister of Education of the Republic of
Kazakhstan (1993-1995)
Member of the Kazakhstan National Academy of
Sciences

PREFACE
RELIGIOUS INFLUENCE IN BUSINESS

Our 21st century global business environment is more geographically and culturally diverse than ever before. With the proliferation of technology worldwide, businesses throughout the world are now interconnected and can transact business with ease. Business professionals must be prepared to engage in this highly diverse business environment. This includes the ability to effectively interact with business professionals of different cultures and different religious affiliations.

Religion plays an integral role in many of the world's cultures. Business professionals must be educated regarding how religious and cultural customs impact business practices in many parts of the world. Because religion is deeply embedded in the norms and customs of society in many countries, it is impractical to claim ignorance when it comes to the religious customs of countries where business professionals will be conducting business. Today's business professionals must be able to effectively navigate the labyrinth of cultural and religious beliefs that permeate the countries where they will be engaging in business.

That's where this book comes in. The intent of the book is to provide business professionals and academics in North America and Europe with a quick and basic introduction to four major world religions: Islam, Judaism, Hinduism, and Buddhism. These four religions represent over four billion people worldwide. Specific countries highlighting these major religions throughout this book include Egypt, Israel, India, and Thailand.

Islam is one of the world's major religions with an estimated 1.8 billion adherents. Islam is a religious and cultural force that needs to be understood by all business professionals who work internationally. Global business professionals will need to understand how Islamic institutions work and how Islamic finance is conducted, since Islamic financial and banking practices differ in significant ways from conventional practices.

There are an estimated 14 million adherents to Judaism throughout the world. Large numbers of Jews are located in Israel, a country with a robust and dynamic economy. Business professionals working in today's global business environment will likely interact with Jewish business professionals who can be found doing business in many countries.

Hinduism is one of the five big religions of the world, with over 1.1 billion followers representing about 15% of the global population. Large numbers of Hindus may be found in India, a country with which the United States does much business. It is highly likely that at some point global business professionals will find themselves transacting business with a Hindu. Therefore, business professionals need to know about Hinduism, its history, beliefs, holidays, practices, and its influence on the business environment.

There are approximately 600 million Buddhists in the world, with the highest concentrations of Buddhists found in the Far East. Buddhist beliefs and practices strongly influence the practice of business in Buddhist areas and between Buddhists and people of other religions.

The material included in the following chapters of this book is adapted from four papers written by the three authors of this book. Dunn and Galloway wrote about Islam, Islamic Finance and Christianity in a paper that appeared in the *Journal of Biblical Integration in Business* in 2011 (Dunn & Galloway, 2011). Dunn and Jensen wrote about Judaism and Jewish Business Practices in a paper that appeared in the *International Journal of Business Administration (IJBA)* in 2018 (Dunn & Jensen, 2018). The paper on Hinduism and Hindu Business Practices was written by Dunn and Jensen in 2019 (Dunn & Jensen, 2019a) and also appeared in the *IJBA*. Finally, the paper on Buddhism and Buddhist Business Practices was written by Dunn and Jensen in 2019, and also published in the *IJBA* (Dunn & Jensen, 2019b).

It is the intent of the authors that this book will give readers a basic understanding of the four religions and the impacts these religions have on global business practices. The target audience for the book is U.S. business professionals. It is assumed that readers already have a basic understanding of business practices in the United States and other individualist countries, and thus the differences in business practices described in this book may be understood as they agree with or differ from U.S. practices.

We begin our comparisons in Chapter 1 with a discussion of Islam and Islamic Business Practices.

This page intentionally left blank

CHAPTER 1

ISLAM AND ISLAMIC BUSINESS PRACTICES

This page intentionally left blank

Introduction

Islam is one of the world's major religions with an estimated 1.8 billion adherents. Islam is a religious and cultural force that needs to be understood by all people of good will, and especially by business professionals who work internationally. International business professionals will need to understand how Islamic institutions work and how Islamic finance is conducted, since Islamic financial and banking practices differ in significant ways from conventional practices. As the world economy becomes increasingly diverse, and as the roles of Muslims and Islamic countries become more important to international trade, it is imperative that business people have a basic understanding of Islamic practices.

Chapter 1 has two principal goals. The first goal is to introduce Islam to the reader. Information about Islam as a religion, its beliefs, history, adherents, and practices will be presented. The second goal is to introduce Islamic finances and banking. A description of Islamic financial institutions will be included, as will background information from Islamic theology and jurisprudence that impacts financial practices. Several Islamic financial instruments will be described.

A note on use of Arabic words. The transliterations of words from Arabic into English create many variations of the same word, such as *Koran* and *Quaran*. It is the writers' intent that the first use of the word coming from Arabic will be italicized but left unitalicized thereafter. The exceptions are *Quaran*, *Allah*, and *Isa* which will always be italicized out of respect. Quotations from another writer will use that author's form.

Islam

The Religion
Islam developed in the sixth century of the Common Era (AD). Islam means "surrendering one's will to the will of Allah." *Allah* is the name for God in Arabic. The first leader of Islam was Muhammad (570-633 AD) who is viewed as the Messenger of *Allah* and the Messenger of Islam. Muhammad was born on the Arabian Peninsula. He gained influence as a business professional and began to spread his ideas in that region. Muslims believe that Muhammad received from *Allah* through the angel Gabriel the message now written in the *Quaran*, the primary holy book in Islam. Muhammad began to gain adherents to his philosophy and theology and became the first proponent of the religion now known as Islam. A description of the expansion of Islam is given next.

History of Islam
The events and dates given in this section are taken from two principal sources. First is the chronology given by Karen Armstrong (2002). The second is the online Islamic History Chronology ("Islamic History," n.d.). Also included is information from the University of Southern California – MSA Compendium of Muslim Texts which was taken from the WinAlim Islamic database ("Chronology," n.d.). Taken together, these chronologies start in 545 AD and end with the start of the war against the Taliban in Afghanistan in 2001. The

following account of Islamic history begins with the death of Muhammad.

Following the death of Muhammad in 633 there were four successive leaders, called Caliphs, of the Islamic world. Their area of influence was largely limited to the areas around the Middle East. In 637 Jerusalem and Syria came under the control of the Muslims. Expanding further, in 639 the Muslims conquered Khuzestan and advanced into Egypt. By 643 they conquered Azerbaijan and Tabaristana. By 659 Muslims had conquered Egypt and Cypress and had campaigned across North Africa ("Islamic History," n.d.).

In 661 a new line of Caliphs came into power, the Umayyed Caliphs, who led for almost 100 years. By this time Damascus was the capital of Islam, and the religion had spread to Central Asia and to the borders of what is modern China to the east and to southern France to the west ("Islamic History," n.d.). During this period the Muslims led campaigns against the Berbers in North Africa and conquered most of what is now Spain. By 725 they were again fighting in France in such cities as Nimes, Tours, and Avignon. They were defeated at the Battle of Avignon in 737.

The next group of Caliphs is called the Abbasids. In 763 the Abbasids moved the capital from Damascus to Baghdad. This caliphate lasted for about five centuries, but the Caliphs gradually lost power to military generals, many of whom were called "sultans" ("Islamic History," n.d.). The Spanish Muslims captured the island of Corsica in 816 and Sardinia and Majorca in 818. In 839 the Muslims conquered Southern

Italy and captured Messina. By 1000 AD Islam had spread into the Indian Peninsula, often accompanied with battles with the Hindus. The Punjab was conquered in 1019.

Not all battles were won by the Muslims. In 1091 the Normans conquered Sicily. It was during this time the Europeans mounted their crusades to reclaim the Holy Land for Christianity. The first crusade was called in 1095, and Jerusalem fell to the Crusaders in 1099. The forces of Islam and Christianity fought in the Holy Land for nearly two hundred years, but Jerusalem itself was returned to Islam when the Kurdish general Salah ud Din captured it in 1187 (Armstrong, 2002, p. 93). The wars continued until the 9th crusade, which ended in disaster for the Christians in 1274.

In the meantime, one of the Umayyed leaders escaped to Spain at the time the Abbasids came into power. The Umayyads established a great Islamic tradition in Spain that lasted until 1492, when the Muslims were finally driven from Spain by Ferdinand and Isabella ("Islamic History," n.d.). For more than 700 years Spain was the center of the world's most advanced civilization.

Muslim Spain was the locus of not only a flowering of Islamic culture, but also of one of the major flowerings of Jewish culture; the close relationship between the two cultures at the time can be seen in the number of works written in Arabic by Jewish thinkers, one of the most famous of whom was Maimonides. Spain also became the most important center from which Islamic learning in the sciences, philosophy, and the arts was transmitted to the Christian West and had such a profound effect on later European history.

By the end of the 13th century the Mongols were on the move. They invaded Syria in 1299 AD and ruled the eastern lands of Islam from India to the Sinai Desert. The conquered people eventually converted to Islam. The leader Timor started a new dynasty in 1360 and ruled that part of the Muslim world from 1369 to 1500 ("Islamic History," n.d.).

The Mongols were replaced by the Ottoman Turks, who gradually came to power in the 15th century. The Ottoman Turks conquered Constantinople in 1453 and basically eliminated the Eastern Christian Empire, known as the Byzantine Empire. The Ottoman Turks gradually conquered Eastern Europe and most of North Africa. The most famous leader was Suleiman the Magnificent, who expanded the empire to Hungary and Austria. The Ottoman Turks remained in power until after World War I ("Islamic History," n.d.).

To the east and south of the land of the Ottoman Turks was Persia. In 1502 the Safavids established a dynasty in Persia that lasted two centuries. Their rule ended in 1736 with an invasion from Afghanistan, which led to the independence of Afghanistan in the 19th century ("Islamic History," n.d.).

Islam gradually extended into India. This expansion halted with the conquest of most of what is now modern India by Babur in 1525. He set up the Mogul empire which lasted, although with decreasing power because of the increase in British power, until 1857. From the 12th century on Islam began to spread to Sumatra, Java, and Indonesia ("Islamic History," n.d.).

Islam spread into the Malay world beginning as early as the seventh/thirteenth century, but especially from the eighth/fourteenth century through Sufi teachers, pious merchants, and a number of men from the family of the Prophet and ruling classes of the Hadramaut and the Persian Gulf who married members of Malay royal families and brought about a conversion to Islam from above.

Indonesia is now the country with the largest Muslim population in the world.

By the year 1500 Islam had largely reached the lands that it now occupies. There was gradual expansion down the east coast of Africa and into the interior of northern Africa, and some gains for Islam in the Orient, but the profiles remain today much the same as in 1500. Part of the slowdown in expansion of Islam can be contributed to the colonization of many parts of the world by the European empires. In that European outreach much of Africa was divided among Germany, Spain, Portugal, Belgium, and England. England gained control of greater India, while the Netherlands, Spain, England, and Portugal gained control of the island states in Asia.

In the 20th century, after the defeat of the Turks in World War I, much of the Middle East came under the control of European countries. Further east the Soviet Empire slowed down Muslim expansion in Central Asia.

The spread of Islam was essentially stopped in India in the 20th century with the portioning of the subcontinent into India, Pakistan, and Bangladesh. Today the Central Asian countries remain mostly Muslim, as are the lands of Indonesia, Malaysia, and the southern Philippines. Also, there are sizable Muslim populations in western China.

Also in the 20th century there was a sizable growth in the number of Muslims in the United States. Many immigrants from the Middle East came to the United States and brought Islam with them. In addition, there has been a significant growth in the number of African American converts to Islam. Many were attracted to the Nation of Islam, a variant on orthodox Islam, which was headed by Elijah Mohammad ("Nation of Islam," n.d.). Malcolm X was a well-known convert to the Nation of Islam, as was Mohammad Ali, the professional boxer. Over the years that movement has gradually moved toward orthodox Islam.

Religious Beliefs and Practices
Islam is viewed as the completion and perfection of earlier religions, especially Judaism and Christianity. The religion is based on the Muslim holy book, the *Quaran*, as well as the life, sayings, and actions of Muhammad.

The word *"Quaran"* means "the recital" (Dawood, 1974, p. 9). The *Quaran* has 114 chapters arranged by length with the longest chapters coming first. It is approximately as long as the New Testament of the Bible.

The words of the *Quaran* are considered by most Muslims to have been dictated in the Arabic language to Muhammad by the angel Gabriel, and hence the words themselves are sacred. Some Muslims believe that only the Arabic words are sacred; translations cannot be sacred. Further, great care must be taken with the material on which the *Quaran* is printed, and Muslims wanting to read the *Quaran* must prepare for touching the *Quaran* with a ceremonial washing.

Earlier holy books from Judaism and Christianity recognized in the *Quaran* are the Book of Abraham, the Psalms, the Torah, and the Gospel of Jesus (Rahim, n.d.). Many of the stories of the Old Testament are repeated in the *Quaran*, often with slightly different details. Many heroes from the Old and New Testaments, such as Adam, Noah, Abraham, Ishmael, Isaac, Lot, Jacob, Joseph, Job, Moses, Aaron, David, Solomon, Jonah, John the Baptist, and Jesus are considered to be Prophets (Rahim, n.d.). Jesus is given special honor, as is Mary, the Mother of Jesus. According to the search engine for the *Quaran* found in the University of Southern California-MSA Compendium of Muslim Texts ("Chronology," n.d.), Moses is mentioned 176 times in the *Quaran*, Jesus is mentioned 28 times, and Mary is mentioned 31 times. The culmination of the prophetic line is Muhammad who has by revelation of *Allah* brought the final word of truth to humankind.

The principal Muslim beliefs and practices are well described in Cragg (1969). First, Islam is a monotheistic religion. There is one God whose name in Arabic is *Allah*. *Allah* is the creator of all that exists. All people of all ages answer to *Allah*. None of the Prophets, not even Muhammad, are *Allah*. *Allah* is eternal (Miles, 2018; Lodahl, 2010).

There are many names of *Allah* which represent *Allah's* attributes (Al-Qazwini, n.d.). Traditionally there are 99 such names which are recited, such as "The

Merciful," "The Holy," "The Creator," "The Just," "The Glorious," "The Trustee," and "The Light."

A second principal belief is that *Allah* is just and abhors injustice. *Allah* is all-knowing and will reward justness and punish injustice.

A third principal belief deals with humankind's freedom to choose good and evil. Muslim opinion is divided on this issue, but the belief that man is indeed free seems to be more in line with the *Quaran*. In this view, humans are free to choose and do good or to choose and do evil.

A fourth principal belief is that there will be a Day of Resurrection and Judgment at which time *Allah* will raise people from the dead, reunite their souls with their bodies, and question them about their beliefs and actions. They will then receive *Allah's* judgment and be assigned for eternity to Heaven (Paradise) or Hell. Paradise is often pictured as a garden with water, plants, and beautiful virgins. Hell is pictured as a place of fire. Both Heaven and Hell have gradations of bliss or punishment.

The purpose of life is to be tested. If one believes in *Allah* as prescribed by Islam, practices the faith, and does good, then one will be ushered into Paradise. If one has done evil, but sincerely repents, then *Allah* may forgive that person and still usher him or her into Paradise.

Despite His ability to destroy mankind if He so willed, the main characteristics of *Allah* are forgiveness and mercifulness, and for this reason Muslims begin nearly every action, speech, or endeavor with the words, "In the name of Allah, the most Merciful, the most Compassionate."

Repentance is a private matter. Further, if a brother or sister Muslim sins, it is important for the knowing Muslim to hide that person's sin as much as possible to preserve their honor and to preserve the honor of Islam.

It is easy to become a Muslim. One repeats the formula "I testify that there is no God but Allah and that Muhammad is the Messenger of Allah." The first successor to Muhammad was the Imam 'Ali, who said that "Islam is submission, submission is conviction, conviction is affirmation, affirmation is acknowledgement, acknowledgement is performance of obligations, and the performance of obligations is good deeds" (Al-Qazwini, n.d., Ch. 2, para. 16).

Muslims have five obligations that represent the pillars of the Islamic faith. First, the Muslim must believe in *Allah* as the sole God and that Muhammad is *Allah's* Messenger. Second is the requirement for prayer. Muslims are required to pray five times every day facing toward Mecca. Third, Muslims must observe the month of Ramadan by not eating food and drink during the daytime. Fourth, Muslims must give alms to those in need. Fifth, unless prohibited by health or finances, each Muslim must make a pilgrimage to Mecca at least once during his lifetime (Rahim, n.d.). [Note: Ramadan in 2019 is from May 6 to June 4. Dates may vary by one day in different countries of the world].

World Muslim Populations

Islam is one of the major religions of the world. At present it is the second largest in terms of adherents, after Christianity. Muslims, or adherents to Islam, may be found in substantial numbers on every continent except Antarctica. Muslim influence appears to be growing as Muslim numbers increase, as countries with significant Muslim populations become more important to the world's economies, and as Muslims seek improved status and recognition in the societies in which they find themselves.

The total number of Muslims in the world is estimated to be 1.8 billion, or approximately 20 percent of the world's population. Using data given in The World Factbook (Central Intelligence Agency, 2018), Muslim populations can be estimated. The countries with the most Muslims are given in Table 1 on the following page.

Three countries which are very important to the United States at the time of this writing are Saudi Arabia, Iraq, and Afghanistan. The first two of these countries have large reserves of oil. Saudi Arabia is a strategic partner of the United States and plays a central role in Islam. Iraq has been center stage since the first Gulf War, and now the United States is winding down a long-term struggle in Iraq after the overthrow of Saddam Hussein. At the time of this writing the United States has been engaged in Afghanistan in a war that is the longest war in U.S. history. Estimated Muslim populations for Saudi Arabia, Iraq, and Afghanistan in 2017 was 28, 37, and 34 million, respectively.

Table 1. Largest Muslim Populations 2017

Country	Number of Muslims (millions)
Indonesia	228
Pakistan	198
India	182
Bangladesh	141
Nigeria	95
Egypt	87
Iran	82
Turkey	81

Note: Data constructed from The World Factbook (Central Intelligence Agency, 2018).

Determining the number of Muslims in the United States is quite difficult. The number given by the World Almanac for Kids in 2008 was 5 million ("Religious Membership," 2008). The Association of Religion Data Archives reported a much lower number following a study in 2000 of the 1209 known mosques in the United States. That study reported 1.6 million adherents, a number considerably lower than the 5 million reported above ("Religious Congregations," n.d.). The study also reported that "33% of Muslims in the United States are of South Asian ancestry, 30% are reported as African American (which would include Blacks from Africa or the Caribbean); and 25% are of Arab descent" ("Religious Congregations," n.d., para. 26). In 2018 it is estimated that Muslims constitute 1% of the U.S. population.

A particularly authoritative study of Muslims in the United States was conducted by the Pew Research Center and published in 2017. This study put the number of Muslims in the United States at 3.45 million. In an earlier Pew Research Center study (2007), it was reported that "72% of Muslim Americans are foreign-born or have roots abroad" (p. 10). Furthermore, it was reported that "most U.S. Muslims (65%) are first-generation immigrants," and "more than a third (37%) of all foreign-born Muslim Americans arrived from the Arab region" (p. 15). "No single racial group constitutes a majority among the Muslim American population: 38% describe themselves as white, 26% black, 20% Asian, and 16% other or mixed race" (p. 17). "Within specific ethnic heritages, 64% of Muslims from the Arab region say they are white, while 20% say they are some other or mixed race" (p. 18).

Many people confuse Arabs with Muslims. Generally speaking, an Arab is a person who speaks Arabic. There are 22 countries which are considered Arabic. Iran, Iraq, Turkey, Pakistan, and Afghanistan, for example, are not Arab countries. An Arab may be an adherent of one of a wide number of religions. It is estimated that approximately 20 percent of the world's Muslims live in the Arab world. Muslims may or may not speak Arabic, although they are certainly encouraged to learn enough Arabic to read the *Quaran*. A 2000 study showed that "only 23% of the Arab population in the United States is actually Muslim" ("Religious Congregations," n.d., para. 36).

The Sunni and Shia Division
Islam was unified so long as Muhammad was alive, but within decades after his death the Islamic world was divided into two major camps: Sunni Islam and Shia Islam. Only 15 percent of the world's Muslims belong to Shia Islam. They are known as Shi'ites. Shi'ites constitute a majority in Iran and Iraq (Murphy, 2007).

The division arose over leadership of the Muslim world. The Shi'ites were led by 'Ali ibn Abu Talib, who was a cousin of Muhammad, the second person to accept Islam, and the husband of Muhammad's daughter, Fatima. "The term Shia or Shi'ite derives from a shortening of Shjiat Ali or partisans of Ali" (Amin, n.d., Sec. I, para. 3). The Shi'ites believe that leadership of the Islamic community should pass from Muhammad to direct descendants of Muhammad through Ali and Fatima (Amin, n.d., Sec. I, para. 4). Each of the legitimate successors carries the title of "Amin" or "Imam" or "Iman," but in recent years the revered ones are called "Ayatollah."

Ali was the first of the Amins recognized by the Shi'ites. Each Amin appointed his successor through twelve Amins, the last of which was Iman Muhammad al-Madhi (the Rightly-Guided One), who was appointed in 873 AD at age four and disappeared within days (Amin, n.d., para. 9). Shi'ites believe that this Iman is still alive. "The Twelfth Imam is still alive. He is in a state of occultation. He will reappear at a moment determined by Allah. He is the Awaited One who will spread justice throughout the world" (Amin, n.d., Sec. III, para. 9).

Following the disappearance of Iman Muhammad al-Madhi and the realization that he was not returning, a council of scholars elected a supreme Iman. The process has continued until this era. Probably the best known of the recent Ayatollahs is the Ayatollah Khomeni, who essentially took over the government of Iran after the fall of the Shah in 1979. Amin writes that the position of the "Shia Imam has come to be imbued with Pope-like infallibility and the Shia religious hierarchy is not dissimilar in structure and religious power to that of the Catholic Church within Christianity" (Amin, n.d., Sec. I, para. 9). "Their imams are believed to be inerrant interpreters of law and tradition" (Amin, n.d. Sec. I, para. 9). The leading Ayatollah at the time of this writing is Grand Ayatollah Ali Sistani of Iraq.

Most Shi'ites are Twelvers, that is, they recognize the first 12 Imans as being legitimate. Another group of Shi'ites are the Ismailis who recognize only the first seven Imans, so they are called the Seveners ("Seveners," 2018). There is a third branch that recognizes only the first five Imans, called the Fiver Shias (Amin, n.d., para. 15).

"Shia Muslims believe that beneath the explicit and literal meaning of the Qur'an are other levels of meaning, which are known only to the imam, who can reveal them to chosen followers." And, "Shia Muslims pay the tax called zakat (originally levied by Muhammad to help the poor and later levied by Muslim states) to their religious leaders rather than to state authorities...As a result, some Shia leaders in Iran and Iraq have immense wealth and property" (Rahman, 2007a, para. 1).

The great majority of the world's Muslims belong to Sunni Islam. This branch of Islam rejected the notion that leadership of Islam should come from descendants of Muhammad. "Sunni Muslims believe that Muhammad intended that the Muslim community choose a successor, or caliph, by consensus to lead the theocracy (earthly kingdom under divine rule) he had set up" (Rahman, 2007b, para. 1). "Sunni Islam, in contrast [to Shia Islam], more closely resembles the myriad independent churches of American Protestantism. Sunnis do not have a formal clergy, just scholars and jurists, who may offer non-binding opinions" (Amin, n.d., para. 9).

Most Sunni and Shi'ite Muslims around the world recognize the other principal group as legitimate followers of Islam. There have been attempts to reconcile differences and to bring more harmony in the world-wide Islamic tradition. However, this has not halted serious dissension and even warfare among Shia and Sunni groups, often not just because of the religious differences but also from ethnic, linguistic and economic competition. A good illustration of one of these conflicts is the situation in Iraq. Sadam Hussein was Sunni and Sunnis controlled most of the important positions in his government, even though Sunni Islam was a minority in Iraq. Currently the Shi'ites are dominant in Iraq and are trying to determine how the Sunnis can best be brought back into the government.

Kharijis and Sufis
Another branch of Islam is the Kharijis, or Ibadi, branch. The Kharijis left mainline Islam, the Sunni branch, in 658 in protest against one of the early Caliphs who this group thought to be an inappropriate leader. They often used violence against people who opposed them. However, "Other than in limited pockets of solidarity they had virtually ceased to exist as a militant sect by 750, and became regarded more as a nuisance strand of fringe intellect" (Jordan, 2002, p. 123).

The Kharijis view the *Quaran* as the principal book to be followed, but place less importance on other writings. They are quite strict and represent a fundamentalist group of Muslims. Today this group represents only about 1 percent of Muslims worldwide. They are most prominent in Oman.

Still another branch is the Sufi movement. The word *sufi* means "wearer of wool" and refers to the rough clothing often worn by members of this group of Muslims. The Sufis are Muslims who want to get closer to *Allah* by living an ascetic life. It apparently had its origins in Iraq near the modern city of Basra between the 7th and 9th centuries CE. It may have been influenced by the Christian monks who lived lives of deep asceticism (Jordan, 2002, p. 124).

Sufis often practice mysticism, and a principal goal is to live a holy life in order to become one with *Allah*. Sufis often flout the Shariah law, for they view that they have risen above the common Islamic law because they are in closer communion with *Allah*. Music and poetry are prized, and many philosophers have come from the Sufi sect (Jordan, 2002, p. 125).

There are many branches of Sufism. A relatively recent branch is the Babis, which originated in the nineteenth century. They believed that the hidden Iman would soon return and bring peace and justice. They led several rebellions and soon got into conflict with the mainstream Shi'ites. This branch still exists in Iran (Jordan, 2002). "Today Sufism is practiced mainly among older age groups of people living in isolated rural communities and is chiefly concentrated in Egypt and the Sudan" (p. 127).

One small but highly visible group of Sufis is the Whirling Dervishes. This group traces its roots to Jalal al-Din Rumi (1207-1273), a Sufi mystic. "Rumi's spiritual and personal life veered from one emotional extreme to another; he sought ecstasy in dancing, singing, poetry, and music, and the members of the order that he founded are often called the Whirling Dervishes because of their stately, spinning, dance, which induces a state of transcendence" (Armstrong, 2002, p. 101).

Additional Sources of Doctrines and Practices
In addition to the *Quaran*, Muslims regard as binding the *Sunnah*, which is the collection of information as to what Muhammad "said, did, or permitted to do" (As-Siba'i, n.d., para. 6). "The Sunan, or 'traditions' of Muhammad, are now gathered in six books, though two of these are more specifically called the Sahihs, or 'sincere books'" ("Medieval Sourcebook," n.d., para. 1). These sayings were gathered over a period of two centuries after Muhammad's death. "Hence, after the *Quaran*, the Prophet's sayings, and his actions are the most important sources of the Law and a fountainhead of Islamic life and thought" (Iqbal & Mirakhor, 2007, p. 15).

The words *hadith* and sunnah are sometimes confused. The hadith are the words and deeds of the Prophet and the Sunnah is the tradition that comes from the words and deeds.

Finally, there are the contributions of Islamic scholars over the centuries. Opinions promulgated by scholars are called *fatwas*. These four, the *Quaran*, Sunnah, hadiths, and fatwas constitute the body of rules called the *Shariah*. The Shariah is highly respected and is binding on all practicing Muslims.

"Unfortunately, Islam is not unified, as described above. There are two major groupings, the Sunni and the Shia, and several smaller groups. Further, each of these main groupings are divided into schools. Today there are five main schools, four from Sunni Islam and one from Shia Islam. The four from Sunni Islam are the *Maliki, Shafi'i, Hanafi*, and *Hanbali* schools. The one from Shia Islam is associated with the Twelvers and is called *Ja'fari*" (Nasr, 2003, pp. 78-79).

Scholars from a particular tradition who have developed the fatwas from the *Quaran*, Sunnah, and Hadiths may have developed laws and rules that differ with those developed in another Islamic tradition. Hence, there is no one Shariah that is binding on all Muslims around the world. This makes it difficult for Muslims and non-Muslims alike to develop uniform approaches to dealing with Muslims in social, religious, and economic matters.

As described above, Shia Islam has the equivalent of a clergy who develop Shariah laws and principles to deal with current situations not covered by the *Quaran* or the Sunnah. Sunni Islam has no equivalent of clergy, so "Sunni Islam relies upon two further sources. One is *Qiyas*, or analogy. By this, the legists argued from the intention of some specific rule of Qur'an or Sunnah, to cover some matter, arguable from, though not stated in, the original" (Cragg, 1969, p. 49). A fourth source is *'Ijma'* or consensus. Founded on the conviction that the community as such would not long, or finally "converge on an error," 'Ijma' in effect entrusted the enlargement of law to the collective fidelity (Cragg, 1969, p. 49). Given these two additional sources for Sunnis, El-Gamal (2006) argued that Sunni Shariah jurisprudence is similar to common law, while Shia Shariah jurisprudence is more similar to civil law.

Some predominantly Muslim countries such as Iran have adopted Shariah law as their legal codes. No Western country has adopted Shariah. Some Muslim communities in the United States use Shariah law as a substitute for conventional law in settling disputes among Muslims.

Islamic Business Practices

Islamic Finances

Some modern Islamic finance practices, particularly the controlling prohibition against charging interest, were also observed in the Christian world until recent times. For centuries Christian scholars argued whether the prohibition was against interest or against usury. Earlier Christian scholars in the Common Era tended to view the prohibition against interest in all forms, but gradually the Biblical literature on this topic came to be interpreted more as a prohibition against usury. Various financial processes, such as the *commenda* contract, were developed to provide financing of entrepreneurial ventures, without charging interest in medieval times. Christians often borrowed money, with interest, from Jewish lenders. When Henry VIII broke from Rome he lifted in 1545 the prohibition against interest, but as late as 1750 Pope Benedict XIV issued the bull *Vix Pervenit* which prohibited all interest, not just usurious levels of interest. Since that time the Roman Catholic Church has dropped its opposition to charging interest, but the problem of interest remains central in Islam (Pollard, 2008).

Foundational Principles

The practice of Islamic finances is based on foundational principles of Islam. One is the principle of stewardship, which states that everything belongs to *Allah*, and humans are to protect the resources that have been entrusted to them and act as vice-regents for *Allah*. Muslims are not to gamble away the resources which they control. Another principle is the concept of justice, which starts with *Allah* as a just God who demands justice of all believers. *Allah* has established rules which will lead to a just society, one in which one person or group does not take advantage of another person or group. It would be offensive to *Allah's* justice and to a just society if one person were to have guaranteed gains coming from an economic activity in which another person might suffer losses. "The underlying principle of Islamic finance is that there has to be a return that is commensurate with the risk involved. There must be risk sharing and an equal-risk reward opportunity rather than having a fixed, predetermined rate of interest" (Trammell, 2005, p. 19).

A third principle is that money is to be a means of exchange, but not a store of value. Muslims are not to make gains just from having money to lend; money must be used for a productive purpose, then gains may be legitimately obtained from that activity. Finally, there is the principle of alms. Giving a loan to another without charging interest is blessed by *Allah*, and it may be that if the borrower defaults on the loan that *Allah* will bless the lender if the loan is forgiven. This last point is driven home in the *Quaran* in 2:276: "If your debtor be in straits, grant him a delay until he can discharge his debt; but if you waive the sum as alms it will be better for you, if you but knew it" (Dawood, 1974, p. 364). Several surrounding verses address the matter of alms in relation to debt.

Muslims can be involved in economic activity only if the activity is not repugnant to Islamic tradition. For example, work with breweries, casinos, and swine farms are prohibited. In today's economy, however, it is often difficult to separate completely from such activities, so the concept of "core business" has been developed. A Muslim may not participate in an economic activity whose core business is prohibited by Shariah. The Five-Percent Rule is helpful here. "The 5 percent rule says that a core business is one that accounts for more than 5 percent of a company's revenue, or gross income" (Trammell, 2005, p. 19).

Extent of Islamic Finances

As Islamic consciousness and influence rise, Muslims around the world are establishing institutions which are congruent with Muslim beliefs. Of particular interest is the growing number of Islamic banks.

An example of a small bank in the United States that caters to an Islamic population near the University of Michigan is University Islamic Financial of Ann Arbor. It advertises on its web site such services as Home Finance, Deposit, Mutual Funds, and Online Services & Forms ("University," n.d.).

As noted above, conventional banks are beginning to pay attention to needs of Muslims. Banks that have established Islam windows include Citibank, the Hong

Kong and Shanghai Banking Corporation, Union Bank of Switzerland, the American Express Bank, American Bank, ANX Grindlays, and Chase Manhattan. A decision Muslim bankers have to make is whether to use Islamic windows to conventional banks, or Islamic subsidiaries, or full-fledged Islamic banks. The Devon Bank of Chicago offers murabaha services ("Islamic Banking," 2017; "Devon Bank," n.d.; Zinser, 2015).

According to a report from the Islamic Financial Services Board in 2016, the "Islamic finance market was estimated to hold assets around $2 trillion" (Kuran, 2018, p. 1307).

Islamic Markets, Indices, and Ratings

Another reason why today's business professional should be acquainted with Islam and Islamic financial practices is the growth of markets for dealing in Shariah-approved stocks and bonds and financial instruments. Islamic bonds are known by the Arabic name sukuk, which will be described more fully below.

Islamic funds are traded on many conventional stock markets. For example, the DJIM Turkey Exchange Traded Fund is traded on the Istanbul Stock Exchange. A few indices have been developed to facilitate the flow of information about securities rising from Shariah-compliant companies. Dow Jones has a bundle of indices known as the "Dow Jones Islamic Market Indices." Several indices are listed including:

DJ Islamic Asia/Pacific Index
DJ Islamic Technology Index
DJ Islamic Market Titans 100 Index
DJ Islamic Market World Developed Markets Index

There are also developing a number of underwriters for Islamic bonds and loans. Traditional rating services are starting to rate certain Islamic banks. For example, "Standard & Poor's Rating Services announced in late September [2007] that it would introduce stability ratings for Islamic banks with profit-sharing investment accounts, or PSIAs" (Platt, 2007, para. 9).

Research, Financial Organizations, and Certifications
In recent years the scholarly study of economics and Islamic practices has grown dramatically. Many research and industry organizations have been established which guide the industry in the development of new Shariah-compliant financial services, in the review of current practices, in auditing institutions, and in attempts to develop services that would be accepted all over the Islamic world. Among such organizations are the Islamic Development Bank (Saudi Arabia), the Islamic Financial Services Board (Malaysia), the International Association of Islamic Banks (Saudi Arabia), the International Center for Research in Islamic Economics (Saudi Arabia), and the International Institute for Banking and Islamic Economics (Cyprus).

The Accounting and Auditing Organization for Islamic Financial Institutions (AAOIFI) based in Bahrain is developing and publishing Shariah standards for Islamic banks in both Arabic and English. The AAOIFI has developed accounting, auditing, governance, ethics, and many Shariah standards. Of particular interest are standards related to capital ratios, foreign currency transactions, disclosure of assets, and Islamic services provided by conventional banks. A complete set of standards may be purchased from the AAOIFI.

The AAOIFI is the sponsoring organization for a professional certification program similar to the Certified Public Accountant certification available in the United States. The Certified Islamic Public Accounting (CIPA) program is now recognized by such banks and organizations as the Central Bank of Egypt and Deloitte & Touche (AAOIFI, n.d.).

Professional conferences related to Islamic banking practices are increasing in number. One such meeting is the Annual Conference on Islamic Banking and Finance.

Shariah-Based Differences in Islamic Economic Activities

To illustrate the complexity of Islamic finance, and in order to demonstrate the need for business professionals to learn more about Islamic finance and practices, a brief excursion into Islamic jurisprudence is warranted. To begin, the rules for conducting Islamic approved business are found in the Shariah. All the rules are based on the theological belief that each economic activity is grounded in the relationship between *Allah* and humans. The form and substance of every economic activity such as lending money, buying and selling, contract law, insurance, buying on credit, use of mortgages, and money markets must all comply with general concepts of stewardship and justice as well as specific rules of the Shariah.

Most economic activities in Islamic financial institutions carry a name derived from Arabic language. This ties the activity to Shariah and emphasizes that the activity is Shariah compliant (El-Gamal, 2006). Each Islamic financial institution has a Shariah board composed of financial and Islamic experts who rule on the compliance of the activities in which the institution engages. As described above, since different Islamic traditions have different Shariahs, what is permitted in one institution may not be permitted in another. Unfortunately, there are not many Muslims who are knowledgeable both about banking and Islam who can serve as experts.

Riba

Two main ways in which Islamic finance differs from conventional finance are in the prohibitions against *riba* and *gharar*. "Islamic finance is a prohibition-driven industry. In this regard, the instigating factor for prohibition-based contract invalidation can almost always be attributed to the two factors labeled *riba* and *gharar*" (El-Gamal, 2006, p. 46). Loosely speaking, riba may be identified as "interest." "[J]urists defined the forbidden *riba* generally as 'trading two goods of the same kind in different quantities, where the increase is not a proper compensation'" (p. 49). Gharar will be described below.

"Literally, the Arabic term *riba* refers to excess, addition and surplus, while the associated verb implies 'to increase, to multiply, to exceed, to exact more than was due, or to practice usury'" (Iqbal & Mirakhor, 2007, p. 54). Like the Christian theologians and scholars over the years, the Islamic scholars have argued whether the prohibition is against interest at any level or just against excessive interest. Almost all Islamic scholars accept that interest at any level is prohibited.

Iqbal and Mirakhor (2007) give another definition of riba as "the practice of charging financial interest or a premium in excess of the principal amount of a loan" (p. 54). Also, "through the prohibition of Riba, Allah (swt) [swt=God of all Gods] has prohibited paying or receiving more than the principal on the money lent as loan irrespective of whether the rate is simple or compounded" (p. 54). Whether the loan is money or some commodity, interest is prohibited whether paid in money or the commodity.

With these preliminary definitions of riba, we can now move to a formal definition, given by Kettell (2010): Technically, it means an increase over the principal in a loan transaction or in exchange for a commodity accrued to the owner (lender) without giving an equivalent counter-value or recompense (*iwad*) in return, to the other party (p. 224). A particularly egregious form of riba is compound interest, in which gain is earned only by the passing of time ("Understanding Riba," n.d.).

In order to avoid riba, Islamic institutions have developed many alternatives that accomplish the desired result for the institution and client. For example, suppose person A (buyer) desires to purchase a house from person B (seller). Further, suppose buyer A approaches Islamic bank C for funds to make the purchase. One approach might be: Bank C purchases the house from seller B. Buyer A purchases a portion of the house from the bank using his or her down payment. Now the bank and buyer A own the house jointly. Buyer A and bank C work out a payment schedule based on the price of the house plus the bank's mark-up, which may very well be based on market interest rates. As buyer A makes payment, buyer A's percentage of ownership in the house increases while the bank's decreases, until eventually buyer A owns the house outright.

Gharar

"Although the word [gharar] itself is not mentioned in the Koran, etymologically related words, meaning deception or delusion are. It is however in a number of Hadiths that gharar is condemned" (Warde, 2000, p. 59).

Gharar comes in several forms, one of which is "the sale of probable items whose existence or characteristics are not certain, the risky nature of which makes the transaction akin to gambling" (El-Gamal, 2006, p. 58). "Generally speaking, gharar encompasses some forms of incomplete information and/or deception, as well as risk and uncertainty intrinsic to the objects of contract" (p. 58).

In simple terms, gharar stems from information problems and refers to any uncertainty created by the lack of information or control in a contract. Gharar can be thought of as ignorance in regard to an essential element in a transaction, such as the exact sale price, or the ability of the seller to actually deliver what is sold, etc. Existence of gharar in a contract makes it null and void.

El-Gamal (2006) quoted the Encyclopedia of Islamic Jurisprudence as listing "cheating (*tadlis*) and fraud (*ghubn*) as special cases of gharar" (p. 59). Gambling is another example of prohibited gharar. In gambling one pays a particular price for the possibility of making a gain that was not obtained by the buyer's use of the resources given to the buyer by *Allah*.

As Warde (2000) pointed out, gharar is not the same concept as risk. "Islam does not even advocate the avoidance of risk. Indeed, incurring commercial risk is approved, even encouraged, provided it is equitably shared. More accurately, gharar refers to aleatory transactions, that is, transactions conditioned on uncertain events" (p. 59). The prohibition against gharar is very strong, but some schools of Islamic thought accept gharar in the case of need.

Examples of activities that are prohibited as gharar include: buying fish that are still in the sea, buying in advance the off-spring that is to come from the stud service of a horse, buying in advance what is in the womb of a cow, purchasing food before it has been weighed, and selling food before having possession of it.

Another consequence of the prohibition against gharar is that gharar cannot be traded. Some believe that the prohibition covers derivatives now used widely in conventional financial markets, for these derivatives are used to transfer risk between and among the parties to the derivative. Further, conventional insurance, when viewed as a sale of safety, cannot be Shariah-compliant (El-Gamal, 2006). "Thus, in both insurance and options, the price (insurance premium or option price) is certain, but its compensation (insurance payment or profit from exercising option) is uncertain, and hence the trade is forbidden based on *gharar*" (p. 62).

Another interpretation of the prohibition is that it prohibits unbundled risk and credit, but not bundled risk and credit. For example, one could buy a cow and its unborn calf, but not just the unborn calf. According to this interpretation, it would be acceptable to buy a warranty on a physical good as part of the sale price.

Having completed this brief explanation of riba and gharar, attention now turns to seven Shariah-compliant economic activities: *mudarabah*, *musharakah*, *sukut*, *murabahah*, *ijara*, Islamic insurance, and credit cards. These descriptions will give the reader further insight into Islamic financial activities.

Mudarabah

A mudarabah is an agreement which brings together an agent with capital to invest (*rabbul-mal*) with another agent (*mudarib*) who has managerial skills to form a partnership to conduct a business enterprise. An agreement is made between the rabbul-mal and the mudarib as to sharing of profits. The rabbul-mal bears all losses unless there is negligence, malfeasance, or misconduct on the part of the mudarib. Normally the rabbul-mal is a silent partner and leaves the running of the business to the mudarib.

Mudarabah contracts are as old as Islam. Muhammad formed a partnership with his wife and acted as a mudarib for their joint enterprises. Mudarabah partnerships bring together labor, capital and entrepreneurship (Jamaldeen, n.d.).

The mudarabah may be limited or unlimited. That is to say, the two agents involved may agree that the business enterprise is limited to a particular industry, or limited to a particular geographic location.

Alternatively, the rabbul-mal may let the mudarib conduct any legal or Shariah-compliant business.

The way profits are to be shared is determined at the beginning of the mudarabah. The division of profits is completely up to the partners and may not be changed unless by mutual agreement. Profits cannot be shared until the rabbul-mal has recouped his original investment. The partnership can be dissolved by either partner. However, the contract is normally time-limited.

Mudarabah partnerships can be formed by juridical people as well as natural people. Further, several agents may band together to be the rabbul-mal for the partnership. Also, these partnerships may be tiered. As can be seen, this type of partnership naturally flows into the work of an Islamic bank, where investors in the bank are the rabbul-mal and funds are provided to various mudarib for business purposes. Alternatively, the bank itself may serve as the mudarib and invest in businesses. Acting as mudarib, the bank should perform adequate screening and monitoring of potential projects worthy of good investment opportunities. In cases where the Islamic bank is acting as the mudarib it may ask for a guarantee or collateral.

Musharakah
A musharakah agreement is similar to a mudarabah agreement. This would normally be called a joint-venture agreement between a financier and a client. The financier may be a person or a juridical person.

There are several types of musharakah contracts. In one type the equity ownership diminishes over time. In another type the ownership is not tied to any particular physical asset.

In recent years the use of musharakah contracts has increased significantly, for it appears that in practice musharakah contracts are quite suitable for long term financing. The government of Sudan has been in the forefront of shifting emphasis toward musharakah financing.

Two objectives have guided [the Sudanese] Government policy in this regard. One objective has been to reduce what de facto was the continuation of interest-based lending through widespread use of synthetic murabaha [discussed below] contracts. Another aim has been to increase long-term finance (Ebrahim, 2011).

Sukuk
Sukuk is the plural form of *suku*. The word sukuk used in the singular refers to an Islamic bond security. Islamic bonds, or sukuk, have been issued since the 1970s, but not successfully until the Malaysian government issued government bonds in 1983. In the 1990s rules were developed which allowed the growth and development of Islamic bonds in Malaysia and Bahrain. In recent years this type of economic activity has grown dramatically.

As noted, government entities started the markets for sukuk. With the success of government-sponsored sukuks, private corporations are obtaining financing through sukuks.

As described above in the discussion of riba, selling bonds purely on the basis of money alone would not be acceptable. However, it is possible to make gains off a real asset. "In other words, the *Shariah* accepts the validity of a financial asset that derives its return from the performance of an underlying real asset" (Iqbal & Mirakhor, 2007, p. 177). Thus, to introduce a Shariah-compliant bond, there must be an asset or bundle of assets to which the bond is tied. The buyer of the bond buys a share in the ownership of the asset and benefits from the gains or losses of that asset.

A sukuk becomes Sharia-compliant through the use of mudarabah, described above. In this instance the entity desiring to sell bonds forms a special purpose vehicle called a Special Purpose Mudarabah (SPM), which acquires assets from the seller to hold and from which proportional ownership is sold to sukuk buyers.

There is one significant difference between sukuk and conventional bonds. In conventional bonds the buyer of the bonds receives guaranteed coupon payments, regardless of the performance of the entity selling the bonds. With sukuk the periodic payments are dependent on the economic performance of the underlying asset (Mohamed, Masih, & Bacha, 2015).

For a fee an investment bank may get involved in the transaction. The bank may provide some oversight and some guarantee on performance. This gives the sukuk more validity and may make the sukuk of investment quality and provide opportunity for trade of the sukuk.

What we have described gives a brief picture of the sukuk process. There are many variations on the theme, some of which are Shariah-compliant and some are not.

A more detailed description of several of these variations is given in their discussion of sukuk.

Murabahah

Murabahah refers to a particular type of contract which is used to purchase goods on credit. If economic person A, natural or juridical, desires to purchase a product from person B, A and B agree on a price. Person A then approaches a financier F, which may be a bank, for funds. Person A agrees to purchase from F the item at the price agreed upon with person B, together with a mark-up to the price of the product. Person A and financier F agree on terms including the mark-up to the cost of the product and on a repayment schedule. Financier F then purchases the product from B, then allows A to use the product. Person A pays for the privilege by paying the financier either on installments or with a lump-sum payment at some specific time in the future. The product itself may serve as collateral for the transaction.

In some cases, person A may act as agent for the financier. It may be that the financier never takes physical possession of a tangible product; the product may pass directly from B to A, even though the legal corresponding sale moves through three entities, B to F to A. One of the questions discussed by the Shariah experts is how much time the financier must hold the product for the entire murabahah to be legitimate. One day? One hour? One second (Gundogdu, 2018; Bazian, 2018)?

Iqbal and Mirakhor (2007) pointed out that in case of a default, "the financier only has recourse to the items financed and no further mark-up or penalty may be applied to the outstanding liability. As opposed to conventional loans where interest keeps accruing, no such accrual takes place in case of *Murabahah*" (p. 89).

A murabahah contract is not a loan, for the financier actually purchases a good which is then used by the entrepreneur to conduct a business activity.

Ijara

An ijara agreement is used when a natural or juridical person wants to lease an asset from another person. The lessee receives possession, but not ownership, of the asset which is then used by the lessor in Shariah-approved activities to gain the usufruct arising from possession of the asset (Kettell, 2010).

There are several requirements to the first use of an ijara agreement to make the agreement Shariah-compliant. Among them are: (1) the activities engaged in by the lessee must not be *haram* (forbidden); (2) the contract terminates at a date certain; (3) assets which can be consumed cannot be leased, such as food, fuel, ammunition, and money; (4) the asset cannot be used for any purpose other than that described in the agreement; (5) the lessee must pay the lessor for any damage to the good caused by negligence or misuse; (6) the lessor may charge a rental fee for use of the asset, the amount of and method of payment for which must be specified in the agreement; (7) the rent begins on the day the lessee takes possession of the asset, and (8) the lease terminates on the day the asset loses its function, if such occurs (Kettell, 2010).

In an ijara agreement the lessor is responsible for maintaining the asset. If insurance coverage is desired, the lessor is responsible for providing for that insurance. The lessor may raise the rental amount to cover insurance costs, but that must be agreed to at the time the agreement is made. With respect to maintenance of the asset, by agreement, the lessor may transfer that responsibility to the lessee who will perform the maintenance for a fee.

As in all Shariah-compliant agreements, interest cannot be charged for late payments of due accounts. However, late-payment fees may be added, if part of the original agreement. Similarly, a discount schedule may be agreed to for early payment of rentals (Kettell, 2010).

Islamic Insurance

For centuries insurance was *verboten* to Muslims. Insurance was viewed as having elements of gambling, betting, and riba. Further, there was a great potential disparity between the premiums paid in and the receipts one might gain from an insurance policy.

In recent years the prohibitions and the stigma associated with insurance have gradually diminished, even those stigmas associated with betting against *Allah*. Now it is even viewed by some as good planning and good risk mitigation, and taking care of one's heirs.

To make insurance acceptable, changes are typically made in the legal relationship between the premium payer and the insurance company. A mudarabah contract is usually used between the buyer of insurance and the company. This allows the buyer to become a partner with the insurance company.

Credit Cards

For many years, credit cards were not permitted for practicing Muslims. That has changed in recent years as Islamic banks are starting to issue such cards. Since riba cannot be charged, other arrangements have to be made.

According to Islamic laws, hadiths and Quran, it is prohibited to pay interest on the money which is withdrawn in advance, like this all the additional interest charges of delaying payment is also prohibited, but if credit card are only served as charge card where you pay the principle amount plus the services charges then its allowed and permitted (Qurabn & Alansari, 2017, para. 14).

Critique of Islamic System

Islamic finance is certainly alive and well in the Muslim world. As shown above, the number of Islamic financial institutions is growing, and the ability of Muslim institutions to serve the Muslim public is steadily increasing. There is no doubt that Islamic financial institutions will increasingly be accepted by the non-Muslim world and will be accepted as full partners in the world economic system. Nevertheless, there are several impediments that are hindering the growth of Islamic financial institutions and practices. Several of these will be described in this section.

First is the lack of agreement whether the *Quaran* is against interest or against usury. Although the majority opinion of Shariah scholars is that interest of any type is forbidden, there is a minority opinion that the better interpretation is that the *Quaran* is just against excessive interest.

One scholar who espoused this minority view is Muhammad Saleem, a Muslim and former President of the Park Avenue Bank of New York. In his book, *Islamic Banking – a $300 Billion Deception* (Saleem, 2006), Saleem argued from other religions, from economic conditions of 7th century Arabia, and from the *Quaran* itself, that riba means usury, not interest. He asserted that Islamic banks are deceptive and dishonest in their practices and actually do charge interest, but under a different name.

Second is the lack of uniformity among Islamic institutions as to which financial vehicles are Shariah-compliant. As noted above, with each institution having its own Shariah board, different rules apply from bank to bank, and country to country. This leaves clients with the difficult task of having to navigate different rules as they work with different Islamic institutions.

Third, there is a lack of sufficiently trained Shariah scholars to serve on all the boards that are needed in Islamic institutions around the world.

The lack of uniform rules makes it difficult if not impossible to develop regulatory systems for Islamic institutions in a country (O'Neill, 2008). In turn, the lack of an Islamic regulatory system impedes trust in the system and increases client risk. Further, the lack of uniform rules makes it difficult to establish performance benchmarks that apply across the industry. However, in countries with regulatory systems that apply to conventional institutions, the Islamic institutions have to meet the conventional regulatory requirements and Islamic rules, thus placing the Islamic institution in double jeopardy (Sharbatly, 2016).

Fourth, there is the matter of cost. As can be seen from a description of several of the Islamic financial vehicles, more steps are often required to accomplish a given financial task. These extra steps take more time and cost more than completing the same task in conventional financial entities. This additional cost has been called the "Islamic premium." While some Muslims may be willing to pay slightly more to be Shariah-compliant, the additional cost still is a hindrance to growth.

The fifth, and not the least, problem is that many of the steps in executing Shariah-compliant financial activities are viewed as a subterfuge to keep from paying riba. From the perspective of the client, the total cost of the service is almost exactly what they would pay if they had to pay interest. Thus, Islamic services often draw ridicule as being hypocritical (Gundogdu, 2018).

The sixth difficulty is described by one Muslim writer who has serious problems with the current financial practice of Islamic institutions. He is Mahmoud Amin El-Gamal, Chair of Islamic Economics, Finance and Management at Riad University. El-Gamal argued that rulings in recent centuries have moved away from classical Muslim jurisprudence, and in doing so *Koranic* social goals are being missed. He argued that by "attempting to replicate the substance of contemporary financial practice using premodern contract forms, Islamic finance has arguably failed to serve the objectives of Islamic Law" (El-Gamal, 2006, p.

xii). Much of El-Gamal's book, *Islamic Finance*, developed this theme with an in-depth study showing how Islamic finance is often inefficient and misses the mark of Islamic theology and beneficial social practice (Ozdincer & Yuce, 2018).

Seventh and lastly, Islamic financial practices will not blossom until they are fully accepted in the United States. This problem was well described in an article by Neeta Thakur (2007) in the *International Financial Law Review* in which sukuk and their acceptance in the United States are discussed. She wrote that "Issuance and demand for sukuk is burgeoning worldwide, but the US, the largest economy in the world, remains an exception" (p. 20).

While these criticisms draw a negative picture, not everything is bleak. First, Islamic services are increasing in extent, so that almost any activity that can be done by a conventional bank can be done by a Muslim institution.

Furthermore, more and more conventional services are being ruled as acceptable to Muslims or conventional services are being slightly modified to become acceptable. An example of the latter is the decision by many Shariah scholars that buyers can act as agents for a financial entity which provides needed funds and can take physical possession of goods bought on time without having the financial entity take physical possession of the good (Saxena, 2018).

Moreover, younger Shariah scholars who are better trained in conventional financial services are entering the scene, and they are more willing to accept conventional approaches as Shariah-compliant. "The essence of this reformative work lies in its attempt to institute a fresh approach to Islamic law and Islamic jurisprudence, one that is harmonious with the Qur'ān and Sunnah as well as real-life experience" (Suzuki, 2016, para. 2).

Fourth, as the number of Islamic institutions grows, as more experience is gained, as information is exchanged around the world, and as transparency increases, more regulatory institutions and benchmark indices have come into existence that increase the trust of the Muslim public which in turn accelerates the growth of Islamic finance.

Consequently, the future of Islamic finance is bright.

Doing Business in Egypt

The Country
The Arab Republic of Egypt (Egypt) has a population of 98 million, of which 90% are Muslims. About 5% of the world's Muslims live in Egypt. Egypt is the third most populous country in Africa. It is a country which is studied to see the impact of Islam on business practices.

Egypt is located on the Mediterranean Sea, at a critical location in northern Africa. Its neighbors are Israel, the Gaza Strip, Sudan, Libya, and Saudi Arabia across the Red Sea. This location makes Egypt a key player in North African and Middle Eastern politics. The nation is approximately three times the size of New Mexico. Critical waterways are the Nile River and the Suez Canal. Only about 4% of the land is devoted to agriculture and 3% is arable. About 95% of the population live within 20 miles of the Nile River.

Egyptian history goes back as far as 3200 BCE. Dozens of dynasties ruled Egypt over the next three millennia, with frequent rule by foreign invaders such as the Greeks, Romans, and Byzantines. Islam and the Arabic languages were introduced in the 7th century AD. The Ottoman Turks conquered Egypt in 1517. The Suez Canal was opened in 1869. The government of Egypt came under the control of Britain, sharing government with the Ottoman Empire. Egypt gained its independence from Britain in 1952. Presidents of the country since 1952 included Abdel Nassar, Anwar Sadat, Sufi Taleb, Hosni Mubarak, Mohamed Morsi, Adly Mansour, and Abdel el-Sisi.

The system of law used in Egypt is most similar to civil law; it is based on penal law and Islamic Sharia law. At the time of this writing the President is Abdel Fattah El-Sisi and the head of government is the Prime Minister, Mostafa Madbouly. The President has a four-year term of office; the next election is scheduled for 2022. The legislature is unicameral with 596 seats, 448 members of which are elected. The remainder are appointed according to quotas for various constituency groups. The Judicial system is headed by the Supreme Constitutional Court which is the final court regarding constitution considerations.

Egypt is a member of the United Nations, the International Monetary Fund, and the World Trade Organization. Egypt's economy was highly centralized during the rule of former President Gama Abdel Nasser but opened up considerably under former Presidents Answar El-Sadat and Mohamed Hosni Mubarak. Agriculture, hydrocarbons, manufacturing, tourism, and other service sectors drove the country's relatively diverse economic activity (Central Intelligence Agency, 2018a).

The Egyptian GDP for 2017 was estimated at $1.201 trillion in Purchase Power Parity. At official exchange rates the 2017 estimate was $237.1 billion. Per capita GDP for 2017 was estimated at $12,700 in Purchase Power Parity. The percentage of the population below the poverty line was estimated at 27.8% in 2016.

United States citizens desiring to travel to Egypt for business purposes will need a visa. A 30-day entrance visa can be purchased online.

Foreign direct investment in Egypt is welcomed. The government has several incentive programs to reduce taxation for foreign entities investing in special industries or sections of the country. Profits and funds may be repatriated from Egypt.

Many forms of business are available in Egypt. Included are: Joint Stock Companies, Limited Liability Companies, Representative Offices, and Branch Offices.

The currency of Egypt is the Egyptian Pound. At the time of this writing the exchange rate with the U.S. dollar is $1=17.8873 Pounds. Foreign currencies can be brought into and removed from Egypt.

Electrification of Egypt is estimated at 99.6%. Fixed-line telephones number 6.6 million and subscriptions to cellular phones is approximately 103 million. Internet users are estimated at 37 million.

Arabic is the official language, but French and English are understood by many in the upper economic classes.

Life expectancy at birth is 73 years. Of the population age 15 and older, 73.8% are literate.

Intellectual property is protected. Patents are protected for a maximum of 20 years. Copyrights for literary, musical, and artistic works are protected for 50 years after the death of the creator. Trademarks are protected forever, with a renewal every 10 years. Designs are protected for a maximum of 15 years, subject to renewal fees after the first 10 years ("Doing Business," 2016).

Non-resident companies are taxed on the Egyptian profits. The typical tax rate on profits is 22.5%. Individual personal income tax is progressive with rates up to 22.5%. There is a VAT of 14%.

Public holidays in Egypt for 2019 are ("Public Holidays," 2019, p. 1):

7 January	Coptic Christmas Day
24 January	Revolution Day
25 April	Sinai Liberation Day
28 April	Coptic Easter Day
29 April	Sham El Nessim
1 May	Labour Day
5-7 June	End of Ramadan
30 June	Revolution Day
23 July	Revolution Day
12-15 August	Eid Al Adha
1 September	El Hijra
6 October	Armed Forces Day
10 November	Moulid El Nabi

Islam

The predominant religion of Egypt is Islam. According to the Constitution other religions are protected; however, there continues to be significant discrimination and acts of violence directed toward non-Islamic adherents. Most Egyptians are Sunni Muslims. There are an estimated 108,000 mosques in Egypt. Sharia law is widely practiced, particularly in matters dealing with individuals.

Many Egyptians are cultural Muslims, not particularly observant of strict Muslim expectations. Nevertheless, foreigners doing business in Egypt should assume their counterparts are observant Muslims until told otherwise or observed.

Islam puts great value on charity. Consequently, there is little shame in begging in Egypt, and you will find beggars everywhere. They compete with taxi drivers, porters, trinket sellers, and others for cash from foreigners.

In accordance with the precepts of Islam, one's destiny is in the hands of *Allah*. Furthermore, Egypt has historically had a stable, static society, in which an individual's job and destiny has been determined by his or her birth. Therefore, the status quo tends to be accepted (Morrison & Conaway, 2006).

Cultural Practices

Family security, family harmony, parental guidance, age, and authority are prized values in Egypt. Harmony, patience, and hospitality in all dimensions of life are prized.

Egypt is a collectivist culture. Relationships are all important. "Business will not proceed until your counterpart decides that they like you. The social side of the deal goes hand in hand with the work-related one" ("Doing Business," n.d., p. 3). Developing the relationship may take several meetings in your country and with your counterpart in Egypt. "Leadership and identity come from a person's lineage and his or her ability to protect the honor of the extended family. This is a kinship culture with little social identity outside the network of kin relationships" (Morrison & Conaway, 2006, p. 152).

Be punctual in your meetings. Your Egyptian counterpart may be late, but you should be there on time waiting for the Egyptian, rather than the other way around. If your counterpart offers to shake hands, go ahead and shake, but remember that you should use only your right hand. Western businesswomen should normally not offer to shake hands. It is good to have business cards ready to pass on to your counterpart; one side of the card should be in English and the other side in Arabic. It is good to look your counterpart in the eye while having a conversation, but do not stare. Direct eye contact is viewed as a sign of trust. Address your conversation partner with his or her official title; if the title is unknown, then use Mr., Mrs., or Miss.

Clothing should be conservative, covering most of the body. Wear the normal business clothes of your country; do not attempt to wear traditional Egyptian clothing. Businesswomen are advised to carry a scarf in case they are in settings where women cover their heads. Be very careful of the use of your shoes, and be especially careful of showing the bottoms of your shoes. Do not cross your legs while sitting in a business environment. Do not wear visible jewelry.

At mealtime do not order pork or alcoholic beverages. The raising and consumption of swine is considered repugnant to Muslims.

You may see two men walking down the street holding hands. This does not mean that the men are gay; it is a customary thing for friends to do. If an Egyptian holds your hand, do not give an indication of distaste.

Exhibit patience when working with your Egyptian counterpart. The pace of business is slower than in the United States or northern Europe. Taking time to build the personal relationship will be one significant time factor that will decelerate the completion of business. In your discussions, don't use high pressure tactics. That doesn't mean you cannot be tough in your negotiations; the Egyptians will typically be tough, but friendly. Be aware that an answer of "yes," does not necessarily mean your counterpart agrees with you; it means he or she has heard and understood your statement and the response is a "maybe."

Do not expect to do business on Fridays, since that is the day for Muslims to have their day of rest and observe religious practices. Many people will not work on Thursday as well. Also, be aware of the large number of national holidays when business will not be conducted. A special time in Egypt is the period of Ramadan, a lunar month-long religious remembrance for practicing Muslims.

The senior male in a business will typically be the decision maker in a business negotiation. Other workers will subordinate their wishes to the leader.

Documents should have two dates, the Western date reference to the Common Era, and the Arabic date. Business hours are typically 8:00 am to 2:00 pm.

Never discuss politics related to the state of Israel. Feel free to discuss the great cultural heritage of Egypt. Sports are normally safe subjects to discuss.

In conversations Egyptians may be loud and boisterous, with many hand gestures given with elbows away from the body. This does not mean the Egyptian is especially emotional; it is a cultural practice. However, the Egyptian will not point at another person.

It is acceptable to bring small gifts to a meeting, but do not bring flowers, since flowers are used at weddings or funerals.

Conclusion

Islam is growing, as is the influence of Islamic business practices. Business professionals who work in global business need to understand the beliefs and practices of Islam. Further, they must understand the workings of Shariah-compliant institutions and be familiar with the principal financial vehicles Islamic institutions use to conduct business.

In this chapter the authors have given a brief explanation of the religion of Islam and described several important Islamic financial tools. These descriptions give information that every business person working in international business should know. It is hoped this discussion will influence the reader to read the *Quaran* and Islamic history, to become acquainted with rules of behavior and etiquette in Islamic countries, and to become familiar with Shariah law as it applies to business.

This page intentionally left blank

CHAPTER 2

JUDAISM AND JEWISH
BUSINESS PRACTICES

This page intentionally left blank

Introduction

Business professionals working in today's global business environment will likely interact with Jewish business professionals who can be found doing business in many countries of the world. The economy of Israel is robust and dynamic, with extensions in many countries. It behooves global business professionals to know what Jews believe and how they conduct business. We begin with a description of Judaism.

Judaism

The Religion

Judaism is simultaneously a culture and a religion. Jews who are religious accept belief in God and observe Jewish law (*halakha*). However, many individuals who identify as Jews do not believe in the religion. Over half the Jews in Israel view themselves as secular Jews and do not follow Jewish religious beliefs or practices.

The United States Supreme Court ruled in the 1980s that the Jews constitute a race so far as some aspects of U.S. law is concerned. However, Jews come from all races, colors and ethnicities, and should not be considered as a cohesive ethnicity.

The world population of Jews is around 14 million. Countries with the most Jewish population are ("Vital Statistics," n.d.):

Israel	6,300,000
United States	5,700,000
Canada	388,000
United Kingdom	290,000

Argentina	181,000
Russia	180,000
Germany	117,000
Australia	113,000

Observant Jews

An observant Jew is one who follows and complies with Jewish law, *halakha*, as contrasted with one who is a Jew by birth or by culture. Exactly what laws are to be followed to be considered observant is ambiguous, but most would agree that following the Sabbath laws and kosher eating laws would be required. The laws, rules, and business expectations described herein are those that apply to observant Jews.

Branches of Judaism

There are three main branches of Judaism considered as a religion: Orthodox, Reform, and Conservative. In the United States "10% consider themselves Orthodox, 18% consider themselves Conservative, 35% Reform and 30% declare no denomination" ("Orthodox," 2016, para. 2). There is also a modern syncretic movement called Messianic Judaism that is noteworthy.

Orthodox Judaism. The most conservative of the three main groups is the Orthodox Judaism branch. Orthodox Jews believe that both the *Torah* and the *Oral Torah* come directly from God (see descriptions of these below). The laws contained in the *Torahs* are to be followed strictly. These laws dictate all matters of life, such as family relations, food, sex, and observance of the Sabbath day. Orthodox Judaism is very conservative in accepting converts; male converts must be circumcised and both men and women must be baptized. There are many branches of Orthodox

Judaism which emphasize different parts of the Scriptures and the laws.

Reform Judaism. The most liberal of the three principal Jewish groups is Reform Judaism. It began in the early 1800s and focused on relief from the strict observance of *halakha*.

While Reform Jews believe in a monotheistic God, they believe the *Torah* and *Talmud* are human products, books written by people who reflected the science and cultural understandings of their times. However, there are principles in the *halakha* that apply to our times. Revelation of truth occurs continuously.

Reform Judaism emphasizes study of the Scriptures, living an ethical life, celebrating the principal life events, survival of Judaism, and living a life of holiness. There is no religious hierarchy in Reform Judaism. Equality of genders is emphasized. Converts are welcome; male converts do not have to undergo circumcision ("B'rit Milah," n.d.). A Messianic Age to come is believed, but not a personal Messiah.

Conservative Judaism. Conservative Judaism is the middle-of-the-road group among observant Jews. Conservative Jews accept that some elements of Judaism must be modernized under the guidance of current rabbis.

Conservative Judaism arose in the 1800s in response to Reform Judaism. Conservative Jews accept the *Torah* and *Talmud* and believe that the *halakha* sets the standards, but believe they should be adapted to modern usages. Not many Conservative Jews follow all the laws all the time, but they still observe most of the kosher and Sabbath laws. Women may become rabbis. Just as among the Orthodox Jews, there are many branches of Conservative Judaism. Conservative Judaism welcomes converts. Male converts must be circumcised and both men and women must be baptized. Conservative Judaism has its greatest followings in the United States.

Messianic Judaism. Messianic Jews are Jews who have accepted Jesus as their personal Messiah. There are an estimated 350,000 Messianic Jews in the world. Many Jews do not accept Messianic Jews as being true Jews ("Messianic," n.d.).

Important Dates in Jewish History

Jewish history is normally assumed to have begun with a man named Abraham. Abraham lived in Ur of the Chaldeans, a city east of the modern state of Israel. The year was approximately 1800 BCE. The principal events in the history of the people of Israel, later called the Jews, with the approximate year(s) of their occurrences follows ("Timeline for the History," n.d.):

Abraham	1810 BCE
Abraham's Tribe to Egypt	1750 BCE
The Exodus Back to Canaan Begun	1280 BCE
Giving of the Law	1270 BCE
Kingdom of Israel	1000-930 BCE
Building of First Temple	970 BCE
Division of Kingdom	930 BCE
Conquest of Northern Kingdom (Israel) by Assyria	720 BCE
Conquest of Southern Kingdom (Judah) by Babylon	585 BCE
First Temple Destroyed	585 BCE
Return of Judah to Canaan	540 BCE
Persian Dominance	540-330 BCE

Temple Rebuilt	520 BCE
Persians Conquered by Greeks	333 BCE
Revolt against Greeks	167-160 BCE
Judah conquered by Rome	63 BCE
Second Temple Destroyed by Romans	70 CE
Jewish Diaspora Begun	70 CE
Rabbinic Judaism Instituted	120-135 CE
Mishnah Compiled/Edited	200 CE
Jerusalem Becomes Part of Byzantine Empire	325 CE
Jerusalem Talmud Compiled	370 CE
Babylonian Talmud Recorded	500 CE
Oldest Existing Text of Full Hebrew Bible	1010 CE
Forced Conversions Begun in Spain	1391 CE
Jews Expelled from Spain	1492 CE
Zionism Begun	1895 CE
Jewish Holocaust	1938-1945 CE
Modern State of Israel Formed	1948 CE

Modern State of Israel

The economy of Israel is quite strong. Israel is a hub for high tech development. The standard of living is similar to that of other western European countries.

In the modern country of Israel there are cultural divisions based on the region from which the citizens migrated to come to Israel. *Sephardic Jews* are those that are descendants of Jews from the Iberian Peninsula and the Spanish diaspora. *Ashkenazic Jews* are those that came from Central and Eastern Europe, although now it typically refers to any Jews from Europe. *Mizahi Jews* are Asiatic Jews, typically from Iraq, Iran and Yemen. Jews born in Israel are often referred to as *Sabras*.

In spite of Israel's geographic location, it does not share many cultural elements with its Middle Eastern neighbors ("Country Comparison," n.d.). The principal reason it is so different from its neighbors is that its culture is shaped by immigrants who have come from all parts of the world, people who generally favor democratic government and lean toward religious Judaism rather than the predominant Arab Islamist tendencies of Israel's neighbors (Tole, 2012).

The six Hofstede indices (Hofstede, Hofstede, & Minkov, 2010; "Country Comparison," n.d.) are:

	Israel	Arab Countries	US	UK
Power Distance	13	80	40	35
Individualism	54	38	91	89
Masculinity	47	53	62	66
Uncertainty Avoidance	81	68	46	35
Long Term Orientation	38	7 (Egypt)	26	51
Indulgence	NA	4 (Egypt)	68	69

Judaism in the United States

There are approximately six million Jews in the United States. About 10% of them are Orthodox Jews. Jews in the United States are full citizens and enjoy all privileges granted to U.S. citizens. Jews hold many leadership positions in government, science, the universities, medicine, and business.

Relationships between Jews and Christians are generally positive in the United States. Notable improvements came after the Catholic Ecumenical Council Vatican II when it became the official position of the Roman Catholic Church that the Jews were not culpable in the death of Jesus. While conditions in the United States are generally positive, there are still occasional acts of violence against Jews and Jewish synagogues.

Jewish Beliefs and Practices

In this section we describe several aspects of Jewish beliefs and business practices. We note that there are not one or two unique beliefs that dominate Jewish practices, such as one would find in Islamic business practices with Islam's prohibition against *riba* (charging interest) and *gharar* (selling products with unknown characteristics). The reader will note that Jewish business practices are congruent with the best business practices found in conventional Western management. We begin by describing the principal Jewish sacred writings.

Sacred Writings
The Torah. The primary sacred book in Judaism is the *Written Torah*. This is the first five books of Moses, sometimes referred to as the Pentateuch; these are the same as the first five books of the Christian Bible. The *Written Torah* contains commandments (the *Mitzvot*) which provide the basic guidance for life's activities ("The Torah," n.d.). The number of these Mitzvot are normally given as 613.

There is also the *Oral Torah* which is a collection of writings believed to have been taught to Moses by God. The *Oral Torah* was maintained in oral form until the 2nd century CE when it was written down in a document named the *Mishnah*. Over time more writings were added in both Jerusalem and Babylon. These additions are called the *Gemara*. In the remainder of this chapter the word *Torah* will refer to the *Written Torah*.

The Talmud. The *Mishnah* and the *Gemara* together are known as the *Talmud*. The word *Talmud* means "learning" or "instruction" in Hebrew. Two versions of the *Talmud* are now recognized: *The Babylonian Talmud* and the *Jerusalem Talmud*. The *Babylonian Talmud* is now the one most used and read. The *Talmud* is divided into 54 sections; each Sabbath day one of the sections is read in the morning service at Jewish synagogues.

The Mitzvot. Contained in the *Torah* are various affirmative and negative rules that every righteous Jew is supposed to follow. These 613 rules must be followed at all times. They cover most aspects of daily life ("A List," n.d.). However, many of these 613 rules applied to Temple worship and the sacrificial system. Since the Temple no longer exists and the sacrificial system is no longer in place, many of the rules have no application today.

In the authors' analysis, 116 of the 613 laws apply to the practice of business ("A List," n.d.). In the sections below dealing with Jewish beliefs and Jewish business practices selected Mitzvot and supporting Scriptures are given. Abbreviations for the various Bible translations used are:

ESV	English Standard Version
GWT	God's Word Translation
HCSB	Holman Christian Standard Bible
ISV	International Standard Version
NASB	New American Standard Bible
NHEB	New Heart English Bible
NIV	New International Version
NLT	New Living Translation

The Hebrew Bible. The *Torah*, the writings of the prophets, and various other writings make up the *Hebrew Bible* (known to Christians as the Old Testament). Sometimes the *Hebrew Bible* is referred to as the *Tanach*. The *Tanach* is divided into three main sections: The *Torah*, the Prophets, and the Writings.

The Midrash. The *Midrash* is a set of writings that contain the commentaries of Talmudic scholars over the centuries.

The Responsa. The *Responsa* are legal decisions, handed down by Jewish scholars and leaders, which provide significant guidance for today's Jewish law. These are not found in one book, but are scattered throughout various sources.

Concept of God

It is believed by some scholars that the concept of God evolved over the centuries of pre-Jewish and Jewish history. In earliest times the predecessors of the Jews believed that every nation had a god. As time passed the Jews came to believe that every nation had its god, but the God of the Jews, *Yahweh*, was the most powerful God. The third concept in this development was the belief by the Jews that there was only one God, their God, *Yahweh*, and all other gods were false gods (Kohler, 2015). Since most of the Old Testament was put in written form after the Exile, this third concept of God dominates the Old Testament.

Yahweh is One, a unitary being. He is incorporeal, and is neither male nor female. He is omnipresent, omnipotent, and omniscient. He created the heavens and the earth and all human, animal and plant life.

Yahweh, God, remains in contact and communication with His human creation.

It is fundamental that God is distinct from creation. "God is not to be identified with anything on earth. This ontological divide is fundamental. God is God; humanity is humanity. There can be no blurring of the boundaries" (Sacks, 2010, loc. 953). Every Jew is to love God, and all of life is to be a reflection of that love. Each Jew is required to recite the Shema two times each day. The Shema is found in the book of Deuteronomy 6:4: "Hear, Israel: The Lord is our God, The Lord is one."

An overriding commandment in conducting business is that God's ways are good and upright, and all business practices must also be good and upright.

Mitzvot: Imitate [God's] good and upright ways. (Deuteronomy 28:9)

The LORD will establish you as a holy people to Himself, as He swore to you, if you keep the commandments of the LORD your God and walk in His ways. (NASB)

The Ten Commandments

Contained in the *Torah* are ten particular commands that were given to Moses by God. These Ten Commandments form the bedrock rules of life and law for the Jewish people. A short version of the Ten Commandments, taken from the Torah, Exodus 20, follows:

You shall have no other gods before Me.
You shall not make idols.
You shall not take the name of the LORD your God in vain.

Remember the Sabbath day, to keep it holy.
Honor your father and your mother.
You shall not murder.
You shall not commit adultery.
You shall not steal.
You shall not bear false witness against your neighbor.
You shall not covet.

Observance of these commandments is required of all observant Jews. The Mitzvot elaborate on these commandments.

The Messiah

Jews do not believe in a personal Messiah who is divine or semi-divine, as do Christians. In order to distinguish Jewish beliefs in a Messiah from Christian beliefs, some Jews refer to the Jewish Messiah by the name *Mashiach*.

"The mashiach will be a great political leader descended from King David (Jeremiah 23:5)…He will be well-versed in Jewish law, and observant of its commandments (Isaiah 11:2-5). He will be a charismatic leader, inspiring others to follow his example. He will be a great military leader, who will win battles for Israel. He will be a great judge, who makes righteous decisions (Jeremiah 33:15). But above all, he will be a human being, not a god, demi-god or other supernatural being" ("Mashiach," n.d., para. 7).

Conservative and Reform Jews generally do not believe in a personal messiah, but instead talk about a messianic age, an age of peace.

Jewish Business Practices

Attitude Toward Wealth and Business

Judaism has a positive attitude toward wealth and business, provided they are used and practiced according to the *Torah* and *Talmud*, which particularly means that wealth must be used to assist the widows, orphans, and the needy in society. High ethical standards must be maintained. Profits in business may be earned provided they do not come at the expense of other people. Diligence and hard work are rewarded by wealth. Proverbs 10:4 states "Lazy hands make for poverty, but diligent hands bring wealth." (NIV)

Corporate Social Responsibility (CSR) and Creation Care

The Torah contains many laws dealing with social responsibility. Many of these deal with business practice; "...there are certain standards of exemplary conduct which...a conscientious business person should consider binding...[C]onduct of business is not exempt from the general commandment to sanctify God's name by dignified conduct in all our social interactions" (Meir, 1996, para. 2).

Managers of publicly held firms who use company funds for socially responsible ends must do so with full disclosure to all stakeholders. Best practice is to make social responsibility a publicly known policy of the firm. A Jewish manager would look to the tithe as a starting point for socially responsible action.

However, Judaism does not necessarily insist on the practice of CSR. Acting benevolently is merely a noble suggestion, since avoiding acts of malevolence is enough to counteract the threat of hell. Whether one goes above and beyond the moral call of duty depends entirely upon free will (Tabory, 1983). While acting maliciously elicits punishment of the soul, acting neutrally, without either positive or negative intent, brings on no such retribution. Still, one would be well advised to act with the welfare of others in mind, since compassion inevitably leads to reward.

The physical universe was created by God. All Jews are to care for and preserve the creation. "...wanton destruction of any kind is a violation of *Torah* law. This is known as the principle of *bal tashchit*...a prohibition against unnecessary destruction or waste" (Friedman, 2001, p. 11). "Wasteful consumption is proscribed by the Torah. Soldiers are not permitted to cut down fruit trees even when besieging an enemy's city (Deuteronomy 20:19)" (Friedman, 2001, p. 11).

Animals are to be treated well. People should not eat until the animals have been fed. Animals are to be rested on the Sabbath, just as people are to be rested. Animals are not to be muzzled when working the fields. Certain animals may be used for food, but they must be slaughtered in a way that does not prolong the suffering of the animal (Genesis 9) (Jacobs, n.d.).

> Mitzvot: Do not muzzle a beast, while it is working in produce, which it can eat and enjoy. (Deut. 25:4)

> You must not muzzle an ox to keep it from eating as it treads out the grain. (NLT)

Business Ethics
Good ethics in business is not found solely by following the Talmud, but rather it is an approach, an attitude, a desire to be good by doing good.

"...the Talmudic sages believed that there is an ethics hierarchy and that individuals should strive to reach the summit...Businesspeople leading their lives according to this principle go beyond the letter of the law and are willing to lose money rather than take advantage of another person's misfortune" (Friedman, 2001, p. 4)

Deception and dishonesty are forbidden. "Any type of deceptive act or practice, including deceptive advertisements and deceptive packaging, would also be a violation of the Biblical principle (Exodus 23:7)" (Friedman, 2001, p. 6).

Vendors must be honest in selling. Hiding faults from the buyer is not permitted and such a sale is null and void. "The Talmud...prohibits such deceptions as: painting animals or utensils in order to fool prospective buyers into thinking they are younger or new; deceiving potential customers by placing the better quality merchandise on top of the bin (and the lower quality merchandise on the bottom...; selling wine that has become adulterated with water in your store without informing the customers" (Friedman, 2001, p. 7).

There are many rules in the Torah and Talmud concerning business conduct. High ethical standards are required of all business professionals. Several of these ethical principles are:

> Mitzvot: Do not wrong a stranger in buying or selling. (Ex. 22:21)

You must not exploit a foreign resident or oppress him, since you were foreigners in the land of Egypt. (HCSB)

Mitzvot: Do no wrong in buying or selling. (Lev. 25:14)

When you make an agreement with your neighbor to buy or sell property, you must not take advantage of each other. (NLT)

Mitzvot: Property may not be stolen. (Lev. 19:11)

You must not steal, you must not tell lies, and you must not deal falsely with your fellow citizen. (NETB)

Mitzvot: Use honest scales and weights. (Lev. 19:36)

You are to maintain just balances and reliable standards for weights, dry volumes, and liquid volumes. I am the LORD your God, who brought you out of the land of Egypt. (ISV)

Mitzvot: Do not lie, cheat, or steal. (Lev. 19:11)

You must not steal. You must not act deceptively or lie to one another. (HCSB)

Other Mitzvot require that excessive markups on necessary goods are prohibited. "Profits from selling necessities such as wheat, wine, or oil are not to exceed one-sixth" (Friedman, 2001, p. 8).

Choice of Leaders
Whether choosing the leader of a country, a judge, or head of a company, people of experience, integrity, and knowledge must be picked. Giving and taking bribes

are prohibited. Leaders are not to acquire an excessive amount of possessions.

> Mitzvot: Leaders must be knowledgeable and experienced. (Deut. 1:13)

> Choose wise and discerning and experienced men from your tribes, and I will appoint them as your heads. (NASB)

> Mitzvot: No one may take a bribe. (Ex. 23:8)

> Do not accept a bribe, for a bribe blinds those who see and twists the words of the innocent. (NIV)

> Mitzvot: That the King shall not acquire an excessive number of horses. (Deut. 17:16)

> Only he must not acquire many horses for himself or cause the people to return to Egypt in order to acquire many horses, since the LORD has said to you, 'You shall never return that way again. (ESV)

> Mitzvot: That he shall not accumulate an excessive quantity of gold and silver. (Deut. 17:17)

> He must not acquire many wives for himself so that his heart won't go astray. He must not acquire very large amounts of silver and gold for himself. (HCSB)

Collecting Interest and Managing Debt

You may charge interest to foreigners, but not to your fellow countrymen.

> Mitzvot: Lending to needy people. (Ex. 22:25)

If you lend money to any of my people with you who is poor, you shall not be to him as a creditor; neither shall you charge him interest. (NHEB)

Mitzvot: Do not make a loan to an Israelite on interest. (Lev. 25:37)

Never collect any kind of interest on your money or on the food you give them. (GWT)

Mitzvot: Lend to an alien at interest. (Deut. 23:20)

You may charge a foreigner interest, but you may not charge your brother interest, that the LORD your God may bless you in all that you undertake in the land that you are entering to take possession of it. (ESV)

Mitzvot: Do not demand from a poor man repayment of his debt, when the creditor knows that he cannot pay, nor press him. (Ex. 22:25-27)

If you lend money to any of my people with you who is poor, you shall not be to him as a creditor; neither shall you charge him interest. If you take your neighbor's garment as collateral, you shall restore it to him before the sun goes down, for that is his only covering, it is his garment for his skin. What would he sleep in? It will happen, when he cries to me, that I will hear, for I am gracious. (WEB)

Managing Human Resources

The business environment continues to evolve and adapt in response to globalization. With the emergence of the global business environment has come a marked shift in human resource management practices. The focus of human resource management has evolved from a primarily administrative function to a strategic function, playing an integral role in the overall success and viability of an organization.

"Religious foundations of human resource strategies are important but are rarely highlighted in the literature" (Ali, Gibbs, & Camp, 2000, p. 118). This is not the case with Jewish practices, for there are several human resource management practices that stem from religious beliefs of Judaism, as well as other world religions. Several human resource management principles can be traced back to the Ten Commandments. For example, the commandment to honor the Sabbath acknowledges that hard work is tiring and rest is needed to rejuvenate and maintain one's health and strength (Exodus 20:10). The importance of time away from work is also acknowledged by many Western countries as demonstrated through labor laws that require organizations to pay workers a premium for hours worked in addition to the regular work week. In the Jewish tradition, all workers are granted a day of rest each week (Perry, 1993).

Many workplace violence policies stem from the commandment "You shall not murder" (Exodus 20:13). Most organizations today have policies in place that forbid violent, aggressive, and abusive behavior among employees. In the Jewish tradition, workers should be protected from harm by employers, as "the Torah obligates [the employer] to make every effort to protect his workers from injury" (Perry, 1993, p. 9).

Sexual harassment and hostile work environment policies relate to the commandment that "You shall not commit adultery" (Exodus 20:14). Just as inappropriate sexual relationships wreak havoc in family life, they are also very disruptive to the organizational environment. "The Torah repeats several times the phrase *lo tikrevu*, meaning 'you shall not draw near.' This is understood by the Talmud to imply a far wider prohibition than the illicit physical relationship itself. Any semblance of inappropriate sexual behaviour crosses clearly defined red lines" (Birnbaum, 2016, para. 8).

The commandments "You shall not steal" (Exodus 20:15) and "You shall not bear false witness against your neighbor" (Exodus 20:16) have encouraged a host of workplace policies related to honesty, integrity, and ethics. Often documented in a Code of Conduct document, organizations outline expectations related to moral and ethical behavior for employees. Policies often include the requirement to be honest and truthful in all business dealings, as well as expectations related to respect of company property and notice that stealing company property is strictly prohibited. Deploying company resources for personal use is also forbidden. "An employee may not use the property of his employer or the employer's firm for his own personal purposes. He must therefore refrain from using the company's telephone, copier, other machinery, car, etc." (Wenger, n.d., para. 7).

There are several Mitzvot that consider the treatment of humans, such as:

> Mitzvot: Do not stand by idly when a human life is in danger. (Lev. 19:16)

Do not spread slanderous gossip among your people. Do not stand idly by when your neighbor's life is threatened. I am the LORD. (NLT)

Mitzvot: A bridegroom shall be exempt for a whole year from taking part in any pubic labor, such as military service, guarding the wall and similar duties. (Deut. 24:5)

If a man has recently married, he must not be sent to war or have any other duty laid on him. For one year he is to be free to stay at home and bring happiness to the wife he has married. (NIV)

Mitzvot: Do not delay payment of a hired man's wages. (Lev. 19:13)

Do not defraud or rob your neighbor. Do not make your hired workers wait until the next day to receive their pay. (NLT)

Mitzvot: He who inflicts a bodily injury shall pay monetary compensation. (Ex. 21:18-19)

If people quarrel and one person hits another with a stone or with their fist and the victim does not die but is confined to bed, the one who struck the blow will not be held liable if the other can get up and walk around outside with a staff; however, the guilty party must pay the injured person for any loss of time and see that the victim is completely healed. (NIV)

Israel A Chosen Nation
A core belief in Judaism is that Jews are a chosen people, chosen directly by God. This choice carries with

it the responsibility to glorify God and be a light and blessing to the nations of the earth. Any Jew who sins brings shame to God and thwarts the country's witness. Deuteronomy 7:6 states: "For you are a holy people, who belong to the LORD your God. Of all the people on earth, the LORD your God has chosen you to be his own special treasure." (NLT)

Judgment and the After-Life

After life on earth is finished, a person's soul will be placed in *Gehinom* (Hell) or *Gan Eden* (Paradise) according to the person's actions while alive. If the person has done more good deeds than bad deeds, then the soul will go to Gan Eden. If the person has done more bad deeds than good deeds, then the soul will go to Gehinom. Psalms 50:6 tells us: "Then let the heavens proclaim his justice, for God himself will be the judge. Interlude." (NLT)

The Torah and the Mitzvot do not speak of hell. The doctrine of hell was developed after the Exile and further in the modern era.

Alms

People with means must share with the poor. A traditional goal is to give 10% of one's income to help people needing resources. The best giving is to forgive a loan. Best of all is helping a person find a job or resources that take the person out of poverty. On the other hand, people should not give away their wealth and destitute themselves in the process. In Deuteronomy 15:7-8 we read: "If among you, one of your brothers should become poor, in any of your towns within your land that the LORD your God is giving you, you shall not harden your heart or shut your hand against your poor brother, but you shall open your hand to him and lend him sufficient for his need, whatever it may be." (ESV)

Kosher Laws

When providing meals for Jewish business professionals, be sure to serve only *kosher* foods, food that is approved to be eaten. Saying that food is kosher means that it is fit and proper to eat. Eating the meat of some animals, such as swine, is not allowed and hence is not kosher.

> Mitzvot: you shall not eat unclean food. Animals acceptable for eating are described in Lev. 11:3: You may eat any animal with divided hooves and that chews the cud. (HCSB)

Certain birds such as pelicans, eagles, owls, and storks may not be eaten. Fish with scales and fins may be eaten; lobsters, shrimp, and crabs are not allowed. Dairy products from non-kosher animals may not be consumed. Milk and meat products may not be consumed together; they may not be cooked together nor served together at a meal. Insects with many legs, and insects with very short legs are not kosher, but four varieties of locust are kosher. All food products that grow on trees, bushes, or plants or grow in the soil are kosher, but they must be examined to make sure they do not contain forbidden insects.

Food utensils must be used only for kosher foods. Any contact with a non-kosher food makes the utensil unclean for use.

The Sabbath and Festivals

The Sabbath is to be observed, as are the holy festivals. No work of humans or beasts is to be done on the Sabbath and specific days of the festivals.

> Mitzvot: Do not work on the Sabbath. (Ex. 20:10)

> ...but the seventh day is a Sabbath day of rest dedicated to the LORD your God. On that day no one in your household may do any work. This includes you, your sons and daughters, your male and female servants, your livestock, and any foreigners living among you. (NLT)

There are several religious festivals that are to be celebrated during the year. Each festival has its own rules about work during some or all of the days of the festival.

> Mitzvot: Celebrate the festivals [Passover, shavu'ot and Sukkot]. (Ex. 23:14)

> Three times a year you are to celebrate a festival to me. (NIV)

Rosh Hashanah is the start of the Jewish New Year. It represents the anniversary of the creation of Adam and Eve, and is a time of inward reflection and preparation for the year ahead. *Yom Kippur* is the Day of Atonement, probably the most important holiday of the year in Judaism. Jewish people traditionally observe this holy day with prayer and fasting, and often spend most of the day in synagogue services. *Sukkos* is the Feast of Tabernacles, which celebrates the gathering of harvest. *Hannukah* is a celebration of the victory of the Maccabees over Syria in 165 BCE. *Purim* celebrates the victory of the Jews over a wicked enemy, Haman, won by the Jewish Queen of Persia named Esther. *Passover* is a week-long celebration of the escape of the Israelites from Egyptian slavery, under the leadership of Moses. *Shvuoth* celebrates the giving of the law to Moses by God on Mt. Sinai.

Synagogue Worship

The Sabbath day is a 25-hour period that begins at sundown on Friday. All three major branches of Judaism respect Sabbath day worship in the synagogue.

Sabbath services normally take place on Friday evening; there may also be a Saturday morning and Saturday afternoon service. The place of worship, the synagogue building, is traditionally built facing Jerusalem. At the end of the synagogue facing Jerusalem there is a raised area on which stands the Ark, a cabinet which holds the Torah. The Torah is typically contained on scrolls. There will normally be a menorah on the raised platform.

Seating will be similar to that of a Christian church. In Orthodox synagogues the men and women sit in separate sections; women sometimes sit in a balcony. In Conservative and Reform synagogues the men and women sit together. Generally, the more conservative the congregation, the more formal the attire. Men may wear a yarmulke and a prayer shawl.

During the service each person will typically have a prayer book which contains readings and prayers in Hebrew and the common language. There will be readings from the Psalms, a recitation of the attributes of God, a recitation of the Shema (Hear O Israel, the Lord our God, the Lord is One), a time for silent prayers, a reading from the *Torah* and other Scriptures, and a chanting of blessings. There may be hymns sung by the congregation, and there may be a sermon which will typically be based on the *Torah* reading of the day (Herman, n.d.; "Synagogue Services," n.d.).

Doing Business in Israel

The two official languages of Israel are Hebrew and Arabic. However, much of business is conducted in English. Approximately 80% of Israeli citizens are Jewish; the remainder are largely Arabs, and most of the Arabs are Sunni Muslims. The following paragraphs deal with conducting business with Israeli Jews. Conducting business with Israeli Arabs will be considerably different (Katz, 2011).

"The Israeli legal system is based in common law, which also incorporates facets of civil law. Israel does not have a formal Constitution. Laws enacted by the Knesset, particularly the Basic Laws of Israel, provide the framework of Israeli law, which is enriched by political and judicial precedent" ("The Israeli Courts," 2014, para. 3).

Business professionals from the United States will typically find their Israeli business partners similar to themselves in orientation and drive, as Israel is increasingly individualistic in culture, and independent decision-making is prized. Israelis want to avoid uncertainty, as illustrated by a Hofstede index number of 81 on Uncertainty Avoidance. They like structure and want things planned out in advance. They do not like to waste time.

"Subjective feelings tend to be the basis for the truth. However, faith in the ideologies of Judaism, including the fact that the state must succeed, problems have to be solved, and security has to be maintained, may modify the truth as one sees it. Objective facts are used to supplement feelings and faith" (Morrison & Conaway, 2006, p. 260).

Men and women are treated almost equally. There can be good camaraderie between bosses and employees. Business partners can be called by their first names. Shaking hands is good. Maintaining good eye contact is appropriate. Exchanging business cards is increasingly done. In business discussion, get straight to the point without being obnoxious. Expect your business partners to be quite direct in communication. Israelis are typically polychronic.

Avoid jokes and too much levity since your Israeli business partner may think you are not serious about your work. There won't be much small talk at the beginning of business sessions. U.S. type gestures are normally acceptable.

Wear a suit until you establish a relationship with your Israeli business partner, then wear clothes similar to those of that partner. Often the business attire of Israel is quite casual, including the wearing of jeans.

Be careful not to get into conversations about political matters, particularly discussions about the Palestinian—Israeli conflict. Whatever the topic, be prepared for a vigorous and maybe even boisterous conversation, with many interruptions of your presentation; this may be unnerving to a U.S. business professional.

Israeli business professionals are typically good negotiators. They would expect several rounds of negotiations and would assume that you, the business professional from the United States, would also prefer extended negotiations. Pressure techniques may be used, such as making final offers, but usually the final offer is not the real final offer. Negotiations may be emotional, and attempts made to make you feel guilty in your bargaining stance. This does not conflict with Jewish beliefs because they likely view your presence at the table means you are not suffering financially.

Be sure to capture all agreements in writing, for the written word is deemed more important that the oral commitment. Expect many details to be placed in contracts. Don't give expensive gifts, for the gifts may be seen as bribery. Stay away from bribery at all costs. Remember that Saturday is the Sabbath for Jews, so don't expect to do business on Saturdays.

Doing Business in Europe

Jewish business practices in Europe are similar to business practices in the United States. However, Jewish business professionals may face more discrimination than they would face in the United States.

European attitudes toward Jews was described by a poll done by the Anti-Defamation League in 2015. A poll was taken in 19 countries, and a discrimination index was developed on a scale of 1-100, with the high number representing the most discrimination. Respondents were asked to respond to such statements as: Jews have too much power in the business world;

and Jews have too much power in international financial markets ("Index," 2015).

Country indices from this poll were: Greece: 67; Italy: 29; Spain: 29; Belgium: 21; France: 17; Germany: 16; and United Kingdom: 12. Turkey, (on two continents), had an index number of 71 ("Index," 2015).

Conclusion

In this chapter the authors provided a brief explanation of Judaism, including an overview of its major beliefs. A review of several Jewish business practices that originate from the traditions and beliefs of Judaism were described. Jewish business practices related to attitudes toward wealth in business, business ethics, corporate social responsibility, and human resource management were shown to be deeply rooted in Judaism. Furthermore, there are specific approaches to conducting business with Israelis as well as conducting business in Europe that can greatly assist business professionals in successfully interacting with Jewish business professionals. These descriptions give information that every business professional working in the global business environment should know. It is hoped that readers will have gained an appreciation for Jews and their beliefs, and as a result, will be better able to navigate the business environment and strengthen business relationships.

CHAPTER 3

HINDUISM AND HINDU
BUSINESS PRACTICES

This page intentionally left blank

Introduction

Hinduism is one of the five big religions of the world, with over 1.1 billion adherents. This represents about 15% of the global population. Countries believed to have 100,000 or more Hindus include Australia, Bangladesh, Bhutan, Canada, Democratic Republic of Congo, Fiji, Germany, Guyana, India, Italy, Malaysia, Mauritius, Myanmar, Nepal, Oman, Russia, Singapore, South Africa, Sri Lanka, Suriname, Tanzania, Trinidad and Tobago, United Kingdom, and the United States. The percentage of the total populations of India, Nepal, and Mauritius that subscribe to Hinduism is 80%, 81%, and 49%, respectively (Central Intelligence Agency, 2018b; Central Intelligence Agency, 2018c; Central Intelligence Agency, 2018d; Hinduism by Country, n.d.).

Our 21st century global business environment is continually shifting, and people from various cultures interact more in the business environment than ever before. At some point it is highly likely that global business professionals will find themselves engaged in business with a Hindu. This is especially true for business professionals working in India, Nepal, Mauritius, or in any of the other country with a large number of Hindus. Therefore, business professionals need to know about Hinduism, its history, beliefs, holidays, practices, and its influence on the business environment. This chapter provides an introduction to the religion of Hinduism and its business practices. Conducting business in India will also be a prominent feature of this chapter, as a large percentage of Indians are Hindu.

Hinduism

The Religion

Hinduism is the oldest of the world's five major religions, dating as far back as 2000 BCE. There is no one founder or originating date for the religion. The religion started in the Indus Valley region, the area now known as India. The civilization of that region and era is also called the *Harappan* civilization. "Some writings of the period have been discovered, but unfortunately in such small amounts that they have yet to be deciphered. Knowledge of this great civilization's religion must therefore be based on physical evidence alone" ("Hindu History," 2016, para. 5). The inhabitants are believed to have spoken a Dravidian language.

History of India

One hypothesis about the history of India is that around 1800 BCE, the Indus Valley was invaded by an Indo-European group known as the Aryans. The Aryans are believed to be responsible for both the Sanskrit language and the Vedic religion. Their religion is thought to be related to Zoroastrianism. However, this perspective on the history of India has been largely discounted by modern scholars as being racist. Scholars say this version of history was imposed by the colonists who perpetuated the notion that nothing good arose inside India; rather, the good and advanced parts of civilization were imported from the North.

Modern scholars generally accept the notion that there was a gradual increase of people from the North moving down into India, from which a new culture emerged. From that time on there was a gradual emergence of Aryan ethnicity. During this era some of the currently known Hindu literature was written down and collected. The notions of Brahmanism arose during this period. Furthermore, the notion of a great male god and mother goddess were recognized. The Vedic texts were starting to be collected. The period from 1500 BCE to 500 BCE is sometimes referred to as the Vedic period.

The Indian caste system was well in place by the end of the Vedic period. In the caste system the people were divided into four main castes: Brahmans (Priests and Teachers), Kshatriyas (Warriors and Rulers), Vaishyas (Farmers, Traders and Merchants), and Shudras (Laborers). A fifth group, the Dalits, were viewed as outcastes; these were street sweepers and latrine cleaners. The main castes were further broken down into about 3,000 castes and 25,000 sub-castes ("What is India's Caste System," 2017).

The next period, from 500 BCE to 200 BCE, is known as the Second Urbanization period. Buddha and the rise of Buddhism is attributed to this period. The theories of *samsara* and *moksha* came into being with their foci on asceticism. This is where urban life began to spread. Towns housed markets, and artisans and merchants began to emerge. During this time iron began to be used in the formation of tools and weapons (Nain, 2018).

The next period is known as the period of Classical Hinduism, from 200 to 1100 CE. During this period the Vedas became the central feature of the religion of most of India. The *Bhagavad Gita* was developed in this period. Ideas about reincarnation and monastic renunciation came into prominence. Hindu temples began to be constructed. Early version of the *Puranas*, such as the *Bhagavata Purana* and the *Vishnu Purana* were developed. Yoga and pilgrimages to holy sites became common.

The next identified period is known as the Islamic Period, from 1200 to 1750 CE. Islam pushed down from the north leading to continuing wars and enslavement of people. In the Northwest of India, particularly in the Punjab, a high majority of the people became Muslim. The leader Babur was born in 1483 and became emperor at age 12 in what is now Uzbekistan. Important Babur conquests were Kabul in 1504 and Delhi in 1526. Babur founded the Mughal Empire, which ruled India for 300 years. He died in 1530 CE ("Babur," 2016).

Following Babur was Akbar the Great. He was born in 1542, a direct descendent of Genghis Khan and Babur. Akbar conquered and ruled territories in what is now Afghanistan, Bengal in the east, and far south in India. He emphasized tolerance and cooperation among his conquered people. Although a Muslim, he tolerated Hindus and married several Hindu princesses. Akbar was a supporter of music and the arts. Akbar died in 1605 CE.

In the 1750s the British Crown gave a monopoly right to the East India Company, which began trading with Indian rulers. In 1765 the East India Company was granted *diwani* – the ability to collect revenue in parts of India. Gradually the East India Company grew so strong that it was the effective ruler over much of what is today northern India. However, growing concern over corruption led to the British Parliament's decision to end East India Company's rule in India, and British Crown rule was established in 1858 CE ("East India Company," n.d.).

"In 1858 CE British Crown rule was established in India, ending a century of control by the East India Company. The life and death struggle that preceded this formalisation of British control lasted nearly two years, cost £36 million, and is variously referred to as the 'Great Rebellion', the 'Indian Mutiny' or the 'First War of Indian Independence'. Inevitably, the consequences of this bloody rupture marked the nature of political, social and economic rule that the British established in its wake" (Kaul, 2011, para. 1).

In 1948 the Indians, under the leadership of politician Mahatma Gandhi, won their freedom from Great Britain. At the time of independence, and with the call of Muslims, the British also created the country of Pakistan in two sections to the Northwest and Northeast of India. The area to the Northeast eventually became independent from Pakistan and was established as the country of Bangladesh.

Science and Mathematics
India made important contributions to the subjects of mathematics and science. Perhaps the most important was the use of a symbol for the concept of zero. This fit in with their introduction of the digital numeral system by which all numbers could be represented by the use of just ten symbols. As early as 500 BCE the Indians had symbols for the numbers one through nine. The Arabs later adopted this system and introduced it to the European world. In addition to the base 10 decimal

system, the Indians started to use a binary system early on for representation of numbers whereby with just two symbols all numbers could be represented (Pal, 2016).

Several other scientific and technical advances are noted. Early on, measurement rulers were introduced by the Harappans to aid in their architectural constructions. In ancient India the scientist Kanad postulated the existence of very small particles, like atoms. These particles could join with other particles to make various substances. The scientists of ancient India knew that the earth is round, it revolves around the sun, and rotates on its own axis. These scientists were able to predict lunar and solar eclipses (Pal, 2016). "In the 700s CE, the Indian doctor Madhav invented inoculation, to prevent people from catching smallpox" (Carr, 2017, para. 11).

Written by Sushruta in 6th Century BCE, the *Sushruta Samhita* is considered to be one of the most comprehensive textbooks on ancient surgery. The text mentions various illnesses, plants, preparations and cures along with complex techniques of plastic surgery. The *Sushruta Samhita's* most well-known contribution to plastic surgery is the reconstruction of the nose, known also as rhinoplasty (Pal, 2016).

India Today

There is still considerable tension, often violent, between the Muslims of Pakistan and the Hindus of India, much of which is centered in the area of Kashmir to the northwest of India. Some want the area to become part of Pakistan, some want it to be part of India, and others want it to be partitioned. Both India and Pakistan are parliamentary democracies with multiple political parties. In India, Hinduism is identified as a strong political force. It is often identified with Indian nationalism over and against more secular and Muslim-oriented political parties.

This brings us to today's Hinduism. Coming from modern scholarship of history, archeology, culture, and the religions of India, the modern notion of Hinduism was born. As Indians and other Asians migrated around the world, they brought with them the Hindu religion and its practices. Perhaps the most popular of these practices is Yoga. It is estimated that over 25 million people in the United States practice some form of Yoga.

Hindu Beliefs

Hinduism is referred to by many as *Sanatana Dharma*, "the eternal law" or the "eternal way" beyond human origins. "Western scholars regard Hinduism as a fusion or synthesis of various Indian cultures and traditions, with diverse roots and no single founder" (Sandip B., 2016, para. 3). There are many variations of the Hindu faith. "Hinduism is one of the oldest known organized religions – its sacred writings date back as far as 1400 to 1500 BCE. It is also one of the most diverse and complex…" (Zacharias, n.d., para. 1).

Who is a Hindu? What does one have to believe to be a Hindu? Those are hard questions to answer since there are so many variations of the Hindu religion. Hinduism can be Monistic, where only one thing exists; this is also known as Sankara's school. Hinduism can be Pantheistic, where only one divine thing exists so that god is identical to the world; this is also known as

Brahmanism. Hinduism can be Panentheistic, where the world is part of god; this is also known as Ramanuja's school. Finally, Hinduism can be Theistic, where there is only one god, distinct from creation; this is also known as Bhakti Hinduism. Hindus can be nihilistic, deistic, or atheistic (Zacharias, n.d.). Jayaram V. (n.d.-b) wrote that: "…Contemporary Hinduism or what people understand as popular Hinduism has a diverse range of beliefs and practices, sects and schools of philosophy, some of which may stand in their own right as religions themselves…Hinduism is difficult to define and cannot be equated with other world religions such as Christianity, Buddhism or Islam" (para. 4).

Hinduism developed over several centuries from many sources, so it is natural that Hinduism has a variety of opinions, practices, and beliefs, some of which are contradictory.

"About the only real issue is whether or not a belief system recognizes the Vedas as sacred. If it does, then it is Hindu. If not, then it is not Hindu" (Zacharias, n.d., para. 4).

Hindus understand the complexity and contradictions of their faith and accept them as part of our existence and its diversity, polarity and duality. The world is made up of dualities. They serve as the framework of knowledge. Hence, whether it is religion, science or any other branch of knowledge, contradictions and diversity of opinion are inevitable in our world. Since knowledge is relative to the context and the perspective in which it is perceived or comprehended, we cannot consider any truth absolute, except those which are declared so in the revelatory scriptures such as the eternal and indivisible state of Brahman or the nature of Self (Jayaram V., n.d.-c).

The difficulty of finding a proper definition is that Hinduism has no central doctrinal authority (similar to the papacy in Catholicism), but it has *swamis* (teachers) or *gurus* (spiritual guides). Today, it is common to identify four different traditions of Hinduism.

Vaishnavism
Vaishnavism is one of the major traditions of Hinduism that comes out of India. People who subscribe to Vaishnavism are known as Vaishnavas, and believe that god is the Supreme all-attractive person, or Krishna. South Asian culture has been greatly influenced by Vaishnava tradition, with contributions to the culture of music, dance, theater, and the arts ("What is Vaishnavism," n.d.).

Shaivism
Shaivism is another major tradition of Hinduism originating in India. Considered the oldest of the Hindu traditions, people who subscribe to Shaivism are known as Saivites, and they worship Siva as the Supreme god. "Saivites believe that the entire creation is both an expression of conscious divinity and is non-different from that divinity which they call 'Siva'" ("Shaivism," 2016, para. 3). Shaivism acknowledges the existence of many other deities, and believe that these deities are expressions of Siva.

Shaktism
Shaktism is another major tradition of Hinduism and its doctrine comes primarily out of the Shaivism tradition. Starting in Northwest India and spreading to

other parts of South Asia, Shaktas, or people who subscribe to the Shaktism tradition, idolize the goddess Shakti (also referred to as Devi). Devi is acknowledged in her several forms as the consort of Siva. "Since Shiva [Siva] embodies the male principle and Shakti embodies the female, the two principles of Shaivism and Shaktism are complementary" ("Shaktism," n.d., para. 2).

Smartism

Smartism is a major tradition of Hinduism that has many consistencies and comingles with the previous three traditions described. Starting in the Common Era, Smartism consists of a synthesis of four philosophical strands, including Mimamsa, Advaita, Yoga, and theism (Smarta Tradition, n.d.). Followers of Smartism are known as Smartas, and are distinguished from other Hindus by their practice of accepting all of the major Hindu gods. As such, they are considered the more liberal and nonsectarian denomination of Hindus ("Four Denominations," 2003).

The appellations are based primarily on the god worshiped as an absolute reality and the traditions that accompany worship of that god (Ramakrishna, n.d.). In spite of its many branches and beliefs, there are certain core beliefs that are common among most branches of Hinduism. These are considered next.

Brahman

The Hindu religion is anchored in the concept of Brahman. Brahman is the highest Supreme god of the Hindu religion. Brahman is considered a single spirit, formless and intangible, from which all things come. "Brahman is the Indestructible and Supreme Spirit. It is present in every atom of creation, but remains there as the Viewer, not affected by creation. The individual soul is a part of *Brahman*" (Brahman, n.d., para. 1).

Hindus believe that Brahman is silent, and exists in and through all things. "In Hinduism, most adherents venerate one or more deities, but regard these as manifestations of Ultimate Reality. The Ultimate Reality that is behind the universe and all the gods is called by different names, but most commonly Brahman" ("Hindu Beliefs," 2016, para. 4). Brahman is similar in many respects to the God of Judaism, being viewed as the single Supreme Being (Brahman, n.d.).

"Most forms of Hinduism are henotheistic, which means they worship a single deity, known as 'Brahman,' but still recognize other gods and goddesses. Followers believe there are multiple paths to reaching their god" ("Hinduism," 2018, para. 2). Hinduism is overwhelmingly considered a polytheistic religion by outsiders. However, most Hindus would argue that their faith is monotheistic. While Brahman is considered the Supreme god of the Hindu religion, Hindus recognize other gods as various forms of Brahman. "Most Hindus are devoted followers of one of the principal gods Shiva, Vishnu or Shakti, and often others besides, yet all these are regarded as manifestations of a single Reality" ("Hindu Beliefs," 2016, para. 3).

Hindu Scriptures

The most ancient of scriptures of the Hindu religion are known as the *Vedas*. The Vedas were written in early Sanskrit and included philosophy, hymns, and instruction for rituals for priests. The *Agamas* are a collection of scriptures from various Hindu devotional schools.

"Hindus believe in the divinity of the Vedas, the world's most ancient scripture, and venerate the Agamas as equally revealed. These primordial hymns are God's word and the bedrock of Sanatana Dharma, the eternal religion which has neither beginning nor end" ("Nine Basic Hindu Beliefs," 2009, para. 2).

The Vedas are comprised of four texts. The *Rig-Veda* represents the knowledge of the hymns of praise for recitation. The *Sama-Veda* represent the knowledge of the melodies for chanting. The *Yajur-Veda* represents knowledge of the sacrificial formulas for liturgy. The *Atharva-Veda* represents knowledge of the magic formulas for the procedures of everyday life (Violatti, 2018).

"The Vedas are more than theology books. They contain a rich and colorful 'theo-mythology,' that is, a religious mythology which deliberately interweaves myth, theology, and history to achieve a story-form religious root. This 'theo-mythology' is so deeply rooted in India's history and culture that to reject the Vedas is viewed as opposing India. Therefore, a belief system is rejected by Hinduism if it does not embrace Indian culture to some extent" (Zacharias, n.d., para. 5).

Souls

Hindus believe that all living plants, animals, and humans have a soul. The soul is eternal, and is part of the absolute soul. Souls have existed from the beginning and will exist forever. Souls are "eternal, indestructible, infinite, pure, all knowing, indivisible and blissful" (Jayaram V., n.d.-b, para. 8). Hindus refer to the soul, or inner self, as Atma. Hindus believe that Atma is in every being.

Karma

Karma refers to the actions a person takes and his or her thoughts during his or her lifetime. If one's actions and thoughts are good, the person has good karma. If one's actions and thoughts are bad, the person has bad karma. Karma is a cause-and-effect principle. A person's karma determines his or her destiny in the next life. "Hindus strive to achieve dharma, which is a code of living that emphasizes good conduct and morality" ("Hinduism," 2018, para. 2).

Interestingly, throughout the world, many people who do not subscribe to Hinduism still believe in Karma. However, a westerner's view of karma is typically not consistent with the Hindu view of karma and the extent to which karma can determine a person's destiny in the next life. "…karma is often misused to denote luck, destiny, or fate. Karma is also misused as a way to explain sudden hardships" (Castro, 2013, para. 3).

Reincarnation

Reincarnation is a common theme throughout all traditions of Hinduism. Reincarnation, which is sometimes referred to as transmigration or metempsychosis, represents the rebirth of the conscious, mind, soul or other entity after bodily death (Reincarnation, 2018).

"Hinduism believes in the rebirth, reincarnation, or transmigration (punajanma) of souls. Souls are born upon earth repeatedly until they achieve liberation. Death is a temporary phase, during which the souls travel to the ancestral heaven and stay there, until they exhaust their karma. Then they fall down to earth and take rebirth. One should therefore not grieve for the dead…What dies in death is the body not the soul. The body is like a garment, which is worn afresh by the soul, whenever it takes birth" (Jayaram V., n.d.-b, para. 15).

The *samsara* concept "suggests a continuous cycle life-death-rebirth where one's current life reflects one's actions in the previous life, and where one's action in the current life reflect one's status in the next life" (Sethi & Steidlmeier, 2015, para. 2).

"Hinduism views mankind as divine. Because Brahman is everything, Hinduism asserts that everyone is divine, atman, or self, is one with Brahman. All of reality outside of Brahman is considered mere illusion. The spiritual goal of a Hindu is to become one with Brahman, thus ceasing to exist in its illusory form of 'individual self.' This freedom is referred to as *moksha*. Until moksha is achieved, a Hindu believes that he/she will be repeatedly reincarnated in order that he/she may work towards self-realization of the truth (the truth being that only Brahman exists, nothing else). How a person is reincarnated is determined by karma, which is a principle of cause and effect governed by nature's balance. What one did in the past affects and corresponds with what happens in the future, past and future lives included" (Zacharias, n.d., para. 6)"

Hinduism believes that human beings are divine and share the qualities and duties of god. Although beings in the mortal world are subject to death and rebirth, they have the opportunity to achieve liberation.

Human beings are endowed with intelligence. Hence, human birth is considered precious and rare. Human beings should avail themselves of this precious opportunity and work for their self-transformation to achieve liberation from the cycle of births and deaths (Jayaram V., n.d.-b).

Heaven and Hell

A minority of Hindus believe there is no hell nor no heaven. A person's future is determined by his or her karma in this life. People with good karma will be promoted to a better life in the next reincarnation. People with bad karma will be demoted to a lesser life, perhaps even a life as a plant or animal, in the next reincarnation.

A majority of Hindus do believe in places called heaven and hell. Most Hindus believe there are several levels of each. People with a majority of good karma will go to one of the levels of heaven after death, while people with a majority of bad karma will go to one of the levels of hell after death. After a period of torture in hell or bliss in heaven, and after the bad karma has been erased, the person will be reincarnated into the next life (Rajhans, 2013).

Stages of Life

In Hinduism, it is believed that human life is comprise of four stages, also called *ashramas*. The first ashrama is known as the *Brahmacharya Ashrama*. This first stage of human life is referred to as the student stage, where one acquires knowledge from his teacher and pledges to remain celibate. The second ashrama is known as the *Grihastha Ashrama*. This second stage of human life is when one enters marriage and has family obligations to fulfill. In this stage, one is to put into practice the skills learned from the teacher during the first stage. The third ashrama is known as the *Vanaprastha Ashrama*. This third stage of human life is when one retires, disposes of their possessions, and enters a life of "entering the forest"– surviving on alms. The fourth ashrama is known as the *Sannyasa Ashrama*. This final stage of human life is marked by complete renunciation and entire dedication to spirituality (Das, 2018; "Four Stages," n.d.).

Meaning of Life

In Hinduism, there are four goals of human life. These include *moksha*, which is enlightenment, *kama*, which is enjoyment, sexuality, and desire, *artha*, which is prosperity, and *dharma*, which is living one's purpose ("Hindu Beliefs," 2016). Dharma is the ultimate goal of life, as it represents one's destiny and purpose. This can also refer to one's occupation, which is often defined by familial class. Another aspect of dharma is paying the five debts.

"Debt to the gods for their blessings; paid by rituals and offerings. Debt to parents and teachers; paid by supporting them, having children of one's own and passing along knowledge. Debt to guests; repaid by treating them as if they were gods visiting one's home. Debt to other human beings; repaid by treating them with respect. Debt to all other living beings; repaid by offering good will, food or any other help that is appropriate" ("Meaning of Life," 2015, para. 3).

Hindu Worship and Temples

Hindus worship their gods and goddesses in many different ways and in many different places. Hindu worship, also referred to as *puja*, typically occurs in the temple, which Hindus refer to as a *Mandir*. However, Hindus may also worship in their home, with some building elaborate sanctuaries and shrines dedicated to their gods and goddesses. Hindu worship is primarily performed in individual settings, as personal offerings play a prominent role in worship ("Worship," 2005). "The giving of offerings is an important part of Hindu worship. It is a common practice to present gifts, such as flowers or oils, to a god or goddess" ("Hinduism," 2018, para. 23).

Proselytizing
Hindus do not normally proselytize aggressively. Since all people have souls, are intelligent, and have freedom of choice, and since there are many paths to god, sincere people should practice the religion they now espouse. Hindus believe that no one should use force to get people to change their faith.

Hindu Festivals and Holidays
There are several Hindu holidays and festivals that are recognized during the year. Dates for the most popular 2019 holidays are:

March 21	Holi: Spring Festival
August 15	Raksha Bandhan: Bond between Brother and Sister
September 2	Mahashivaratri: Festival of Shiva
September 29	Navaraatri: Adlebration of Fertility and Harvest
August 23	Janmashtami: Krishna's Birthday
October 27	Diwali: Festival of Lights

These dates may be changed by a few days in individual countries ("Hindu Holidays," n.d.).

Who is a Hindu?

Some of the main beliefs of the Hindu religion have been discussed in this section. To understand any religion fully, one must commit to a lifetime of study. The authors' goal here was to give the reader a broad overview of Hindu beliefs for purposes of preparing business professionals to engage in business effectively with Hindus. The lingering question that can come from this condensed description is, so who is a Hindu? Jayaram V. (n.d.-b) described it as such: "Truly speaking, a Hindu is not just a follower of Hinduism or a particular religion. It does not even matter, whether he is a follower of Hinduism or not. Any person who is a seeker of truth and who is interested in knowing the truth of himself and his existence is a Hindu, whether he believes in God or not, whether he is a Hindu or a Buddhist or a person of some other faith. A Hindu is an individual soul who has been separated from God, is under illusion and has been in the process of rejoining God someday. No one need to force him to become a Hindu in the physical sense, because one day, in some birth, he will become aware of what he is or who he is. What he does in between is all part of a Divine Play" (para. 21).

Next, the authors discuss how Hindu religious beliefs and culture manifest themselves throughout business in an effort to prepare business professionals to effectively engage with Hindus in our 21st century global business environment.

Hindu Business Practices

Hindu beliefs about business and government arose over the centuries; much of the basic philosophy was set at least 20 centuries ago and was extended and preserved in the ensuing years. One early writer with much influence to this day was the politician and economist Kautilya Arthashastra who wrote about 300 BCE (Grinaru & Iavorschi, 2013).

Arthashastra laid down many principles that influence today's business and political practices. First, he thought there should be a strong government with a strong leader, and that leader should increase the wealth of the state and his own power. Part of the manner in which that can be accomplished is for the leader to master the four sciences: state leadership, economics, the Vedas, and philosophy. This philosophy about state leadership moves over into corporate leadership, promoting strong leadership in the highest levels of an organization.

He also promoted the idea of international trade. His concept involved the idea of comparative advantage, anticipating Adam Smith by 2000 years. To him imports were as important as exports.

Arthashastra's other principles included monopolies were to be discouraged; prices and profits were to be kept fair; there should be a tax system which would have reasonable rates, should be inexpensive it its administration, does not negatively impact economic growth; and there should be high taxation on luxury goods. Another principle maintained that laborers should be given fair wages, depending on their skills and productivity.

Business Ethics

When it comes to business ethics, viewpoints vary widely throughout the business world. Business professionals derive their own personal morals and ethical beliefs from various places, a prominent one being their religious beliefs (Head, 2006). Hindu business professionals are no different. Ethical considerations are highly important in Hinduism. Among other considerations, this involves making a distinction between what "is" and what "ought to be."

What Chattopadhyay (2012) writes about India applies to Hinduism as a whole: "Ethics as an institution of life has been recognized here from the very early age of the Vedas. Rather it has been recognized as the most basic element in human life. But then it has not necessarily been recognized as a social enterprise in the sense of being an instrument of the society to help guide the people living in the society. It is rather engrained in the very being of the universe. Ethics has a divine origin. Man has simply to adopt from there" (p. 114).

Ethics are determined at the individual level. If each individual in a business firm is ethical, then the firm will exhibit ethical behavior. "A man of character…is ready to give up his life, but not truth. He is prepared to die, but will not kill. He is willing to accept suffering, but not inflict it on others. He does not seal, nor takes bribes. He does not waste his time or that of others, goes on doing his duty fearlessly" (Chattopadhyay, 2012, p. 120).

The Gita, which captures the essence of Hindu teaching and philosophy, is influential in Hindu business practice. "The Gita's essence…provides the keys for influencing contemporary management thought and global business practices…Karma refers to developing a detached involvement by doing one's duty objectively without worrying about the consequences. And Tat-Twam-Asi is the recognition of the interconnectedness of nature, the human, and the spiritual. It encourages managers to look at the big picture, a holistic view, for guidance with a realization that there can be no simultaneous winners and losers. When managers change their outlook, success is enhanced" (Natesan, Keeffe, and Darling, 2009, para. 4).

The five restraints (truthfulness, not to steal, non-violence, sexual moderation, non-possession) and the five observances (surrendering to god, satisfaction, purity, austerity, self-knowledge) of Hinduism inform the practice of business (Ramakrishna, n.d.).

Patron god of business professionals is the Lord Ganesha, who is represented as an elephant. "Ganesha's elephant head makes him easy to identify. Ganesha is widely revered as the remover of obstacles, the patron of arts and sciences and the deva of intellect and wisdom" (Sandip B., 2016, para. 5). Each of the body parts of the typical representation of the elephant has meaning. For example, the large ears tell us to listen more. The small mouth tells us to talk less. The small eyes tell us to concentrate on our work. The large stomach reminds us to digest well all the bad and good in life. The trunk shows us to be adaptable and have high efficiency.

While Hindus pursue wealth as do people of other religions, it is understood that wealth does not by itself bring happiness. Hinduism does not specifically object to acquisition of material wealth. It is however mandatory that such wealth must be obtained righteously and it must also be shared and distributed. Personal gain is not the main purpose of work. The work done should benefit all of society and therefore when it pertains to the fruits of that work, and individual should only keep what is necessary, and distribute the rest (Bennett, Guillen, Nelson, Olsen, Smart, & Waller, 2010).

Respect for elders is a foundational element of Hindu culture and business practice. Juniors show deference by sitting to the left of elders, never arguing or challenging them in public, and not sitting while an elder is standing. This has implications for reporting legal and ethical issues in business.

Hindus believe purity is a requirement of a person's personal and professional life. "Purity is another vitally important trait in Hindu culture. Hindus believe that one must reach purity of three forms: mind, speech, and body or sometimes referred to as thought, word, and deed" (Bennett et al., 2010, para. 2).

In the Hindu tradition, religion and work are inextricably linked. "Religion tends to have a great effect in the way individuals approach the workforce and on the work they choose to do. For Hindus, doing work that has divine and spiritual significance generated greater satisfaction and commitment in continuing to do said work. Helping others is seen as a way to serve God" (Bennett et al., 2010, para. 36).

Helping others occurs throughout business on a regular basis. In the truest sense of customer service, business professionals engage in helping people through providing products and services to meet their needs.

"Serving the customer is equated with serving God. The Gita is neither a practical guide-book of moral efforts nor a philosophical treatise discussing the origin of immoral tendencies and tracing them to certain metaphysical principles as their courses; but, starting from the ordinary frailties of attachment and desires, it tries to show how on can lead a normal of duties and responsibilities and yet be in peace and contentment" (Chattopadhyay, 2012, p. 116).

The Gita also considers that the person and the person's job should be aligned. No single person can do all jobs. Business managers must discern the skills and abilities of each worker and assign that worker to a job the worker can handle. Workers so assigned must work with a good attitude. Managers and workers must practice the seven duties of "forgiveness, self-control, non-stealing, steadiness, truthfulness, wisdom, and learning" (Chattopadhyay, 2012, p. 117).

Business governance must exhibit the five basic human values of peace, love, truth, righteousness, and good conduct. Leaders of businesses must know him or herself, and must manage him or herself before managing other people.

Conducting Business in India

History of India
When India achieved its independence from Great Britain in 1947 the government set up a state-centered

economy based largely on socialist principles following the Soviet model. Social systems were put in place to help the poor. Heavy industry was encouraged. There were high taxes put on imports and foreign direct investment was discouraged. A burdensome state bureaucracy was put in place which stifled entrepreneurs and the growth of business.

During the first 45 years after independence, India's economy was divided into two distinct segments, private and public. The private sector owned and operated small to medium size businesses and industries protected by the government and the government took care of everything else. The government was in charge of most of the consumer services including transportation such as airlines, railroads and local transportation, communications services such as postal, telephone and telegraph, radio and television broadcasting, and social services such as education and health care.

The intention of the government was to provide these services, at a reasonable cost, as well as employment. India adopted a five-year development plan from its closest ally, the Soviet Union, in order to improve infrastructure, agricultural production, health care, and education. But the progress was extremely slow due to India's democratic system (Gosal, 2013).

After four decades on this model, it became apparent that the system was not working to the advantage of the people and the economy. Poverty had not been significantly reduced. Beginning in the early 1990s the national government started to introduce reforms that made it easier for businesses to thrive.

Import taxes and bureaucratic red tape were reduced. New laws began to allow foreign companies to invest in the country. Liberalization and privatization became the order of the day.

Two other changes should be noted. First, laws permitting Indian companies to invest outside the country were introduced, and second, a growing middle class increased domestic consumption. By the end of the 1990s, the Indian GDP was rising at an annual rate of 5% or more; that rate of growth is still being reached 20 years later (Gosal, 2013).

India Today
The Republic of India/Bharatiya Ganarajya (India) is the seventh largest country in the world by land mass, with the second largest population of approximately 1.25 billion people. It is a federal parliamentary republic whose capital is New Delhi. There are 29 states and 7 union territories. Common law as modified is the system of law practiced in the country. The Prime Minister at the time of this writing is Narendra Modi, who has been Prime Minister since 2014. The country works under a Constitution that was last modified in 2015. There are many national and state political parties. The parliament is bicameral. The Council of States has 245 members and the People's Assembly has 545 seats. The country's Supreme Court has a Chief Justice and 25 Associate Justices (Central Intelligence Agency, 2018b).

Agricultural land constitutes nearly 61% of the land mass, with nearly 53% arable. Forests cover 23% of the land mass. Nearly 33% of the population is urbanized. Life expectancy at birth is 67.6 years for men and 70.1

years for women. Overall literacy in India is 71.2% (Central Intelligence Agency, 2018b).

India's GDP (Purchase Power Parity) is $9.459 trillion and $2.611 trillion at the official exchange rate with the U.S. dollar. The economy's growth rate is estimated at 8.2%, 7.1%, and 6.7% for the years 2015, 2016, and 2017 respectively. Agriculture is the largest sector by employment, encompassing 47% of the workforce. Industry represents 22% of the workforce, and services represents 31%. Approximately 21.9% of the population live below the Indian poverty line. Military expenditures were estimated at 2.47% of GDP for 2016 (Central Intelligence Agency, 2018b).

Compared to most developed countries, income tax rates are quite low in India. At the time of this writing the exchange rate between the US dollar and the Indian Rupee was $1=69.78 INR. Income tax rates for men below 60 years of age in FY 2017-2018 were ("Taxes," 2018):

Income Level	Tax Rate
Income up to 250,000 Rupees:	0
Income between 250,001 and 500,000 Rupees	5% of Income Exceeding 250,000 Rupees
Income between 500,001 and 10,000,000 Rupees	20% of Income Exceeding 500,000 Rupees

The two primary languages spoken in India are English and Hindi. There are also an additional 14 official languages. However, there are over 400 other languages spoken throughout the country. The foreigner traveling to India for business purposes must be prepared to engage a translator for detailed work in many parts of the country.

Singh and Sharma (2013) in their article *India Lacks Business Ethics* paint a poor picture of business ethics in India. They particularly warn tourists to be aware and watchful. "From airports to taxis, hotels, shops and tour guides–all try to fleece innocent tourists (more so if they are foreigners) in a country that claims to practice *atithi devo bhava* (a guest is likeGod (sic)). It has tarnished India's image as a favoured tourist destination. Growing sexual assaults against women tourists worsen the already bad situation" (Singh and Sharma, 2013, para. 7).

The following perspective on Indian business practices was shared in the article *Ethics and Business*: "...*Global Economic Crime Survey 2016*, for instance, says 94 per cent of the Indian respondents stated that their organization had a clear code of conduct, yet only 15 per cent indicated that their leaders walk the talk" ("Business and Ethics," 2016, para. 1).

Religions in India

Approximately 80% of the population of India are Hindus, 14% are Muslims, 2.3% are Christians, and 1.7% are Sikhs. Sikhism is a relatively new religion, having started about 600 years ago. Sikhism is a monotheistic religion that draws its tenants from Hinduism and Islam. There are about 27 million Sikhs worldwide of which 83% live in India. The religion is strongest in the Northeast in the Punjab region. Most male Sikhs have a middle name or surname of Singh. "Sikhs believe in reincarnation but do not recognize caste distinctions. Unlike Hindus, Sikhs reject nonintervention with the world as cowardly" (Morrison & Conway, 2006, p. 225).

Companies in India

One will find in India the same types of companies that exist in most developed countries. There are sole proprietorships, partnerships, limited liability partnerships, family owned businesses, one-person companies, and various types of corporations. One unusual type of corporation is the Hindu Undivided Family (HUF) business. In the HUF only family members can manage and own the business.

Corporations in India have the typical characteristics: separate property, independent corporate existence, perpetual succession, limited liability, capacity for suits, access to money markets, professional management, and government registration. Corporate law is governed by a series of laws, the most recent being the Companies Act of 2013 (Srivastava, 2018).

Hindu Law

The legal system of India recognizes the special needs of people who practice the Hindu religion. To this end a system of laws was passed that apply to Hindus regarding marriage, adoption, inheritance, and other personal matters. Laws concerning these matters include the Hindu Marriage Act, the Hindu Succession Act, the Hindu Minority and Guardianship Act, and the Hindu Adoptions and Maintenance Act. These laws were adopted in the 1950s and remain in force today ("Hindu Law," 2017). There is a comparable set of laws for Muslims while Sikhs are placed under Hindu law.

Because India is largely Hindu in its religious orientation, it is important that business professionals understand key elements of practice in India. As one can determine from the discussion below, the Hindu culture permeates all aspects of business practice.

"At an intellectual level, Hindu religion provides both a basis for moral values and a prescriptive mode that influences one's conduct and actions. This flexibility in interpretation allows Hindus to adapt to different religions and mores. This approach has led Indian's leading companies to imitate the conduct of their foreign MNCs and adopt the exploitative practices for their own benefit while bemoaning the poverty and misery of the masses as their manifest destiny (Karma)" (Sethi & Steidlmeier, 2015, para. 3).

Business Protocol
In addition to a Passport, you may need a visa if you are visiting India for business purposes. If you are going to remain in India for any length of time, you will need to register your presence with a Registration Office.

India has a collectivist and high context macro-culture. In this type of culture, relationships are all important. Business professionals must develop a first-person relationship with their counterparts if they are to enjoy long-term success doing business in India. In staring a business relationship, it is good to have a third party make the introductions.

When meeting with another male, it is important to offer a handshake. When meeting a female, it is important to wait until she offers the handshake. Among themselves, on meeting Indians will often use the *namaste*, which is a gesture where the palms of the hands are brought together at chest level, together with a modest head bow. The namaste is also used as a gesture for goodbye. The word is understood to mean, "I bow to the god within you."

Business professionals must have their business card ready to present. Business cards should reflect information in English on one side and in Hindi on the other. Business professionals must treat business cards received from counterparts with much respect, as this contains the person's name and title, both of which constitute the personal brand of that person.

Business meetings in India will often be accompanied by tea or a soft drink. Business professionals should be sure to partake of the drink, and be prepared for refills. At mealtime, business professionals should typically refrain from ordering meat dishes.

It is generally acceptable to eat with your hands. In many homes and restaurants, you may not be provided with food utensils. One should only use his or her right hand to access the food. If your hand is dirty from eating, do not use the hand to access the serving spoon; let the host serve you.

Most Hindus in India are vegetarians, but being vegetarian is not required of Hindus. Because of the possibility that another human being has been reincarnated into an animal which is being offered as food, most Hindus are reluctant to eat the meat of that animal. It is prudent for business professionals to order a vegetarian meal when eating out with a Hindu business professional, at least until one has determined that he or she is not a vegetarian.

Business practice in India is hierarchical in nature. Organizations are structured with a clear hierarchy and chain of command, and authority is retained at the highest levels of the organization. Decision-making is largely executed from the top down. Considering their preference for retaining authority for top leaders, it would be prudent for business professionals to include leaders from the highest levels of the organization when visiting India to conduct business.

As a high context culture, words and word choice are very important. Business professionals must be exceedingly careful with their speech. One must be very polite to the business counterpart. One should use their official title often in the conversation. Also, avoid saying "no" to any proposal, but use some other phrase such as "that is an interesting concept and I will give it serious thought."

Don't bring gifts of any significant value to a business meeting. High-value gifts may be considered as bribes, which is sure to damage the business relationship. Also, be careful in the choice of colors of any gift or gift-wrapping. White flowers are used at funerals in India.

The family is very important to most Indians. Families in many parts of India still engage in the practice of arranged marriages, and separation and divorce rates are very low. There are myriad of family-owned businesses throughout the country as well. Business professionals should do their homework and thoroughly get to know the people and the businesses they plan to engage in business with.

Business professionals should not expect to do any business on holidays or religious observance days. In particular, Hindu business professionals observe the following holidays: Holi, Raksha Bandhan, Mahashivaratri, Navaraatri, Janmashtami, and Diwali ("Hindu Holidays," n.d.).

Business Attire

Dress and attire are much different in eastern countries than in western countries. "The distinction between ordinary dress and religious dress is difficult to delineate in India because the ordinary members of the various socioreligious groups may often be distinguished by their costumes" ("Types of Dress," 2018, para. 1). In particular, Hindu men will often wear an *angarkha*, which is a short dress coat, and Hindu women will often wear a *sari*, which is a long scarf. Business professionals from the western world need not adhere to the religious or cultural attire of the east when on business; however, one should dress in a professional manner.

Business attire will normally be more formal in India than in the United States. Men should dress in formal business attire; a business suit is appropriate. Formal business attire also works well for women; a pantsuit is acceptable in all parts of India. If a female business professional wishes to wear a skirt, it should be longer in length, and cover the knees when seated (Carson, 2018). Many Indian women are wearing western attire, a growing trend throughout the country (Chatterjee, 2014). Neither men nor women should wear clothing that reveals too much of the body.

A unique aspect of clothing in India is head coverings. Hindu men rarely wear turbans. If a man is wearing a turban, he is most likely a Sikh. In some cases, particularly in sacred spaces, Hindu men may wear a cap or other head covering, but usually not a turban. Hindu women mostly wear a drape, known as a sari, over their head, and some wear veils over their face (Choate, 2013).

Business professionals should avoid postures that are considered aggressive, such as placing hands on the hips or crossing arms. Also note that the feet are considered unclean, much like the left hand. It is prudent to refrain from discussing national or regional political topics such as discussions about relationships between India and Pakistan. One should also avoid discussions about nuclear weapons or about religious doctrine.

Although the caste system is outlawed in India, it is still a significant part of the culture. People of different castes attempting to do business together may find it difficult.

Human Resource Management

Organizations in India work hard to attract, develop, and retain quality employees. Branding is important for Indian companies, as they leverage their unique branding initiatives not only for marketing purposes, but also for attracting high quality applicants. Indians prefer to work for distinguished companies with good branding, even if it means accepting a lower salary. Employee referrals are highly regarded, and a person's ability to secure employment with a distinguished company is often predicated on whom he or she knows in the industry. While employee referrals are not necessarily a prerequisite to being considered as a potential employee by a company, it surely accelerates the screening process (Rao, 2015).

After securing employment with a company in India, one can expect to receive training and development from the organization. Similar to western culture, high performance is rewarded with increased remuneration, promotions, and other fringe benefits. Organizations also reward high performers by giving them preference in choice of projects and jobs performed. Larger organizations are becoming savvy at creating future workforce profiles and succession planning (Rao, 2015).

Retaining employees is a top priority for organizations in India. Organizations employ a variety of strategies to retain high-performing employees, including skill development, career development, and effective employee relations strategies. Organizations understand the importance of employee empowerment and its effects on employee engagement. One of the biggest employee engagement initiatives currently is training of supervisors and managers to effectively work with employees and extend retention efforts (Rao, 2015). Lack of training for managers has been identified as a significant issue in American organizations, with nearly 60% of managers in a recent study reporting that they receive no training at all (O'Donnell, 2018).

Emphasis on work-life balance is growing phenomenon in India, with many organizations already moving in that direction. Recent studies have revealed that many employees in India place higher value on work-life balance, even if it means lower pay. Organizations are also reaping the benefits of employees achieving a better work-life balance. "One of the most important aspects of work-life balance is understanding that it is a key factor to ensure well-being of employees–a core component driving performance" (Mukherjee, 2017, para. 4).

Similar to western countries, India has a host of employment laws aimed at protecting the health, safety, and rights of Indian workers. There are laws regarding employee health and safety, trade unions, minimum wage, equal pay, worker's compensation, and many more. In recent years, India has come a long way with regard to employee leave benefits. For example, women can take up to 26 weeks for maternity leave depending on family size and longevity of employment–far longer than the amount of time women in the United States receive. Furthermore, there are provisions in law for paternity leave benefits for government employees, and legislation aimed at granting paternity leave for private sector is being considered (Aich & Mathias, 2018; "Maternity Leave," n.d.).

Some of India's most recent employment laws relate to sexual harassment. The law requires Indian employers to implement policies that prohibit sexual harassment, and require annual filings of sexual harassment claims. Furthermore, the law requires organizations to establish a committee to hear sexual harassment complaints. "The committee must be chaired by a woman, at least half of its members must be women and must have one independent member who must have expertise in sexual harassment matters or matters relating to women" (Aich & Mathias, 2018, para. 51).

Due to the culture's respect for authority and for seniors in the society, whistleblowing is not common. While the Whistleblower Protection Act was passed in 2011, it really only applies to public servants and governmental entities. Therefore, consistent protections for whistleblowers are loose, and enforcement is lax. "Many instances of fraud, bribery and corruption do not get reported for the fear of retaliation…" ("Business and Ethics," 2016, para. 2).

Conclusion

Organizations today continue to break through geographic and cultural barriers as they expand their reach in today's global business environment. Recent research suggests that this trend will only continue into the future, with 57% of small businesses confident in their global operations while 63% claim that they are experiencing "good-to-booming" global growth ("New Data," 2017, para. 1). Business professionals engaged in the global business community will benefit greatly from learning about the various cultures and religions of areas of the world where they may do business. Considering the highly globalized nature of the business environment, and the increasing presence of south-central Asian countries such as India, it is highly likely that a global business professional will conduct business in this region with Hindu business professionals at some point.

CHAPTER 4

BUDDHISM AND BUDDHIST
BUSINESS PRACTICES

This page intentionally left blank

Introduction

Buddhism is one of the major religions of the world, with its adherence encompassing about 8% of the global population. Buddhism is most prevalent in Thailand but also has a strong presence in many areas throughout the world, including China, Japan, Korea, Singapore, Vietnam, Cambodia, Laos, Sri Lanka, and Burma. Other countries that are heavily influenced by Buddhism include Tibet, Bhutan, Mongolia, surrounding areas in India, China, and Russia ("Demographics of Buddhism," n.d.). Buddhism has some presence in the United States as well, with the highest concentration of Buddhists residing in Hawaii ("Buddhists," 2019).

This chapter explores Buddhism and considers how Buddhist beliefs influence business practices in Thailand and abroad.

Buddhism

Buddhism is a world religion that originated more than 2,500 years ago. Buddhism began in India in the 5th century BCE, and has grown over the centuries to become one of the major religions of the world. Approximately 470 million people around the world subscribe to the Buddhist religion; most of its followers are concentrated across East and Southeast Asia. However, in recent years, the religion has expanded its influence throughout the West ("Buddhism," n.d.). In the United States, Buddhism continues to grow and is expected to reach more than 4.2 million followers by 2020 ("An Asian Religion," 2018).

History of Buddhism

Siddhartha Gautama, also known as the Buddha, was believed to have been born circa 624 BCE (alternate date is 563 BCE) in Lumbini, a location near the Himalayas (Vail, n.d.). Born to royalty, the Buddha was brought up in a wealthy home with many luxuries. However, as he grew older, he began to take notice of human suffering and became disillusioned with the pleasantries of life. He therefore took steps to renounce his splendid lifestyle and banished himself to the forest almost to the point of starvation. He turned to meditation, and at some point attained enlightenment, also known as Nirvana (Vail, n.d.).

At this point the Buddha, which means "the enlightened or awakened one," began to share with others this compassion for suffering. He dedicated the remainder of his life to teaching his vision of *The Middle Way* and instructing people how to achieve enlightenment. "Rather than severe mortification of the body or a life of indulgence insense pleasures the Buddha advocated a moderate or 'balanced' wandering life-style and the cultivation of mental and emotional equanimity through meditation and morality" (Vail, n.d., para. 5).

The Buddha began sharing his beliefs widely and delivered his first sermon near Varanasi (a town in India). "This was a key moment in the Buddhist tradition, traditionally known as the moment when the Buddha 'set in motion the wheel of the law'" (Violatti, 2013, para. 15). From there, the Buddha began to accumulate disciples, and he continued spreading his teachings throughout northern India for about 45 years. While on his deathbed the Buddha encouraged his disciples to continue spreading the vision that they had dedicated their lives to living.

Upon his death the Buddha's followers continued his teachings, and organized a religious movement, which laid the foundation for what would become Buddhism. The disciples continued to encourage teachers, and the Buddha's philosophies and teachings continued to spread primarily throughout northern India for the next 200 years or so. In 268 BCE, Ashoka the Great became the ruler of the Indian Mauryan Empire, and after an aggressive and bloody campaign to expand his kingdom, became remorseful and converted to Buddhism (Merryman, 2018). Ashoka the Great then declared Buddhism to be the official state religion of India. He sponsored the widespread development of many monastic schools and monasteries (Vail, n.d.). "He used the Buddha's dharma to reform his government and sent Buddhist missionaries throughout India, Sri Lanka, Southeast Asia, China, and North Africa" (Merryman, 2018, para. 17).

Over the years Buddhism continued to spread throughout the East. "Buddhism however was not bound by the restrictions of the Hindu caste system and therefore more suitable for the world outside the peninsula" (Hesselink, n.d., para. 5). In the first century CE, Buddhism spread to Central Asia and China. This was about the time the Buddha was first represented in art as in human form. Statues and sculptures were constructed in areas with heavy Buddhism influence. In the second and third centuries CE, Buddhism expanded to Burma, Cambodia, Laos, Vietnam, and Indonesia.

Over the next several centuries, Buddhism continued to spread throughout Southeast Asia, and eventually found its stronghold in Thailand in the tenth century CE. Around that same time, Islam began to spread quickly throughout Central Asia and eventually replaced Buddhism in many Central Asian countries ("Timeline of Buddhist," n.d.).

The spread of Islam throughout the tenth and eleventh centuries CE eventually led to a decline of Buddhism in India. However, Buddhism was continuing to spread throughout Southeast Asia at a rapid pace. Buddhism flourished in Korea under the Koryo Dynasty in the twelfth century CE. It wasn't until the nineteenth and twentieth centuries CE that Buddhism spread beyond Southeast Asia and began moving across Europe and to the United States ("Timeline of Buddhist," n.d.).

The growth of Buddhism had a profound impact on the world and could be visibly seen through art and architecture throughout the East, with notable structural and cultural presence in Indonesia, Vietnam, Laos, Sri-Lanka, and all throughout Southern Asia (Hesselink, n.d.). "Buddhism became a powerful cultural influence in Asia and has remained the majority religion for thousands of years" (Merryman, 2018, para. 17).

Today there are many forms of Buddhism practiced around the world. The three most predominant forms of Buddhism are region specific, and include Theravada Buddhism, Mahayana Buddhism, and Tibetan Buddhism. Theravada Buddhism is primarily practiced in areas of Thailand, Sri Lanka, Cambodia,

Laos, and Burma. Mahayana Buddhism is prevalent in China, Japan, Taiwan, Korea, Singapore, and Vietnam. Tibetan Buddhism is most common in Tibet, Nepal, Mongolia, Bhutan, parts of Russia, and northern India ("Buddhism," 2018). The country that is most heavily influenced by Buddhism is Thailand.

Thailand

The country with the largest Buddhist population is Thailand. "The official religion in Thailand is Theravada Buddhism, practiced by more than 95% of the population and by many who reside in Laos, Myanmar, and Cambodia" (Iverson, 2017a, para. 3). The influence of Buddhism throughout Thailand is pervasive. Many majestic temples can be found throughout the country, along with many spirit houses and other signs and symbols of the religion. Many ornamental shrines and statues of the Buddha grace the country. "The Buddha is considered sacred in Thailand, so any disregard for even an image of Buddha is considered disrespectful. Visitors should not touch, point, or sit higher than any of the Buddha images found in temples throughout Thailand" (Iverson, 2017b, para. 5).

Some 300,000 Buddhist monks reside in Thailand. Monks, also known as *bhiksu* (Sanskrit) or *bhikkhu* (Pali), are usually recognized by their bright orange robes, although some Monks wear robes of different color. Monks usually reside in Buddhist Monasteries and have dedicated themselves to a life of meditation and study. As with other religions, traditions have changed over the years. "In modern times, it is not unheard of for ordained *bhikkhus* and *bhikkhunis* to live outside of a monastery and hold a job. In Japan, and in some

Tibetan orders, they might even be living with a spouse and children" (O'Brien, 2018, para. 20).

We will now consider some of the major tenants and beliefs of Buddhism in an effort to prepare business professionals to effectively engage with Buddhists in the 21st century global business environment.

Buddhist Beliefs

Siddhartha Gautama was born in 624 BCE (alternate date is 563 BCE) in Lumbini, which is now part of Nepal. When he was 29 years old he began to realize there was pain, suffering, and poverty around him. This caused him to spend many years fasting, meditating, and praying as he tried to understand the truths of life. He finally realized many truths after gaining enlightenment, or *nirvana*. He left home, became a wandering holy man, and began to teach those truths to people around him. As a result, he was given the title of *Buddha*, or Enlightened One ("Buddhism: Basic Beliefs," n.d.; White, 1993). The principles he taught are called the *Dhamma*, or Truth.

The Buddha's Teachings

The Buddha taught these truths for the rest of his life. He gained many converts to his way of thinking. After decades of growth the followers of his teachings wrote down the truths in summary form. The core truths were found in the lists known as the Three Universal Truths, the Four Noble Truths, and the Eightfold Path. The Buddha urged the people not to worship him as a god.

Three Universal Truths. One of the principal teachings of the Buddha is called the Three Universal Truths. The

Three Universal Truths are:

> Everything in life is impermanent and always changing.
>
> Because nothing is permanent, a life based on possessing things or people doesn't make you happy.
>
> There is no eternal, unchanging soul and "self" is just a collection of changing characteristics or attributes.

Buddhist acknowledge these truths as integral beliefs of their faith.

Four Noble Truths. Another principal teaching of the Buddha is called the Four Noble Truths. The Four Noble Truths are:

> Human life is suffering.
>
> Suffering is caused by greed.
>
> Suffering can be overcome and happiness achieved.
>
> The way to end suffering is to follow the Middle Path.

The way of the Middle Path is the way to nirvana. People following the Middle Path do not lead lives of indulgence or luxury, but also do not do too much fasting or living lives of hardship. The Eightfold Path gives guidance for people following the Middle Path.

The Eightfold Path. Another principal teaching of the Buddha is the Eightfold Path. The Eightfold Path incorporates the following concepts:

> Right understanding and viewpoint
>
> Right values and attitude

Right speech
Right action
Right work
Right effort
Right mindfulness
Right concentration and meditation.

The Five Precepts. Although Buddhism has splintered into many sects, all Buddhists follow the five precepts which give guidance for daily living:

Do not harm or kill living things.
Do not take things unless they are freely given.
Do not carry on sexual misconduct.
Do not speak unkindly or tell lies
Do not abuse drugs or drink alcohol.

The Buddha's teachings continue. After the Buddha's death at the age of 80 his teachings were collected and written down. A collection of the Buddha's sayings is called the *reipitaka*, or Three Baskets. The name of Three Baskets for the Buddha's sayings came from the early practice of writing on palm leaves which were then gathered in baskets ("Buddhism: Basic Beliefs," n.d.).

Meditation

Most Buddhists practice some form of meditation. The goal is to look within oneself to seek the truth and to understand the truths of the Buddha. The goal of the meditation is to achieve nirvana, or enlightenment. The state of enlightenment cannot be put in words—it surpasses words.

Meditation means focusing the mind to achieve an inner stillness that leads to a state of enlightenment. Meditation takes many forms:

It can be sitting quietly beside a beautiful arrangement of rocks, contemplating beauty.

It can be practicing a martial art such as karate or aikido since they require mental and physical control and strong concentration.

It can mean focusing on a riddle such as "What is the sound of one hand clapping?"

It can be contemplating a haiku or short poem that captures a moment in time.

It can be in a meditation room of a monastery.

It can involve chanting.

It can involve the use of a mandala to focus attention to the invisible point at the center of interlocking triangles.

It can involve quietly noticing one's breath as it goes in and out. It can happen anywhere at any time ("Buddhism: Basic Beliefs," n.d., para. 9).

Idols

Most Buddhist religious centers will have a statue of the Buddha. A typical pose for the Buddha is sitting with hands resting in his lap. Many times the statue will be covered in gold. Buddhists do not worship the Buddha, but venerate his memory. Buddhists are not to ask favors of the Buddha in prayer. Gifts are often left at the site which are then used by Buddhist monks.

The Law of Dependent Origination

The Buddha is attributed with finding the law of dependent origination, or *paticca-samuppada*. "One condition arises out of another, which in turn arises out of prior conditions. Every mode of being presupposes another immediately preceding mode from which the subsequent mode derives, in a chain of causes" ("Buddhism," 2019, para. 25).

What Is the Self?

The Buddha taught that what we think of as our "self" – our ego, self-consciousness and personality – is a creation of the *skandhas*. Very simply, our bodies, physical and emotional sensations, conceptualizations, ideas and beliefs, and consciousness work together to create the illusion of a permanent, distinctive "me."

The Buddha said, "Oh, Bhikshu, every moment you are born, decay, and die" (O'Brien, 2019, para. 5). According to O'Brien (2018), what the Buddha meant in this statement is: "He meant that in every moment, the illusion of 'me' renews itself. Not only is nothing carried over from one life to the next; nothing is carried over from one moment to the next. This is not to say that 'we' do not exist – that there is no permanent, unchanging 'me,' but rather that we are redefined in every moment by shifting, impermanent conditions. Suffering and dissatisfaction occur when we cling to desire for an unchanging and permanent self that is impossible and illusory" (para. 5). Release from that suffering requires no longer clinging to the illusion.

The Buddha taught that all things are dynamic, and in a state of constant change. Things are "always changing, always becoming, always dying, and that refusal to accept that truth, especially the illusion of ego, leads to suffering" (O'Brien, 2019, para. 7).

Ten Realms of Being

Buddhists believe there are 10 realms of being. These are the levels of existence in the universe. The ten levels are divided into two sections, the first section incorporating six of the ten levels, and the second section incorporating four levels.

The first six levels are:

> Hell or Jigokudo
> Hungry Ghosts or Pretas
> Animality or Chikushodo
> Anger or Shurado
> Humanity or Jindo
> Heaven

The top four levels are:

> Learning or Shomon
> Realization or Engaku
> Bodhisattva or Bosatsu
> Buddhahood

The levels are ordered, with the top level of the second section being Buddhahood. Human existence is one of the first six levels. If people do not rigorously seek Buddhahood they will remain in one of the first six levels (Gannon, 2017; Lee, 2016).

Concepts of God

There is no concept of a personal God in most branches of Buddhism. Buddhism believes in the existence of neither God nor soul in the theistic sense. It is essentially a religion of the mind, which advocates present moment awareness, inner purity, ethical conduct, freedom from the problem of change, impermanence and suffering, reliance upon one's own experience, and discernment on the Eightfold path as the teacher and guide, rather than an external authority other than the Dharma. "Buddhism is not centered on the concept of God as the upholder and sum of all or a universal supreme being, who is responsible for the creation and dissolution of the world and the existence of sentient beings" (Jayaram V, n.d.-a, para. 2).

Reincarnation

"Reincarnation normally is understood to be the transmigration of a soul to another body after death. There is no such teaching in Buddhism. One of the most fundamental doctrines of Buddhism is *anatta*, or *anaatman — no soul* or *no self*. There is no permanent essence of an individual self that survives death, and thus Buddhism does not believe in reincarnation in the traditional sense, such as the way it is understood in Hinduism" (O'Brien, 2019, para. 1).

"A gross misunderstanding about Buddhism exists today, especially about the notion of reincarnation. The common misunderstanding is that a person has led countless previous lives, usually as an animal, but somehow in this life he is born as a human being and in the next life he will be reborn as an animal, depending on the kind of life he has lived" (Tsuji, n.d., para. 2).

This is an important topic to Buddhists that is often misunderstood by outsiders. "This notion of the transmigration of the soul definitely does not exist in Buddhism" (Tsuji, n.d., para. 6).

"When Buddhism was established 2,500 years ago, it incorporated a revised Hindu belief in reincarnation. Although Buddhism has two major subdivisions and countless variations in regional practices, most Buddhists believe in *samsara* or the cycle of rebirth. Samsara is governed by the law of karma: Good conduct produces good karma and bad conduct produces evil karma. Buddhists believe that the soul's karma transmigrates between bodies and becomes a 'germ of consciousnesses' in the womb. Periods of afterlife, sometimes called 'the between,' punctuate samsara, coming after death and before rebirth" (Dowdey, n.d., para. 1).

"Like Hindus, Buddhists see unenlightened samsara as a state of suffering. We suffer because we desire the transient. Only when we achieve a state of total passiveness and free ourselves from all desire can we escape samsara and achieve nirvana, or salvation. Many Buddhists believe an individual can end the cycle of reincarnation by following the Eightfold Path, or middle way. An enlightened being embodies the directives of the Eightfold Path: correct view, correct intention, correct speech, correct action, correct livelihood, correct effort, correct mindfulness and correct concentration" (Dowdey, n.d., para. 2).

For readers who are in cultures which have concepts of soul coming from Christianity or Islam, the question arises: If to the Buddhist there is no soul, what is it that transmigrates from physical life form to succeeding form? The answer is that it is life itself that transmigrates. Life is above the world; it is supramundane. Living physical beings such as humans or animals or plants participate in that life. As the material person or animal or plant dies the life in which that person or animal or plant shared continues on and may become associated with another person, animal, or plant.

Buddhist Numerology

The reader will have noticed that many things are numbered in Buddhism. There are the Four Noble Truths, the Eightfold Path, The Five Precepts, etc. Numbers are important to Buddhists, not just because of their explicit meanings and use in counting of objects. Numbers also have unconscious or hidden meanings, or refer to historical events, or refer to an important life principle; these numbers help us understand our lives.

"Number is part of the universal language of symbolism. The spectrum of connotations of numbers is similar across different cultures, but as always, what is actually said in this shared language may be quite different. For example, the symbolism of 'One' is shared between Buddhism and Vedism, but while the Vedas yearn to return to the One, Buddhists seek to let go of the One so as to realize the only truly Buddhist number – zero" (Sujato, 2010, para. 20).

Buddhist revere numbers as the meaningful symbols they can be. For example, exploring the first four counting numbers, the number one represents cosmic unity. The number two represents the division. "The original primordial Being splits into 2 beings, which simultaneously desire and oppose one another. Day/night, male/female, left/right; the world of binaries and oppositions come into being" (Sujato, 2010, para. 11). The number three represents integration of the Divine and the profane, while the number four is the number of completion, encompassing, perfection and balance (Sujato, 2010).

Branches of Buddhism

There are many branches of Buddhism. Since Buddhism does not require adherence to a particular creed, as it spread around the globe regional differences emerged as Buddhism meshed with local cultures. Over 20 main branches of Buddhism have been identified. Two main branches are the Theravada School and the Mayahana School.

Theravada School. One of the major branches with many sub-branches is the Theravada School. This school traces its origins to a council of Buddhist followers that took place about 100 years after the Buddha's death. "Employing Pali as their sacred languages, the Theravadins preserved their version of the Buddha's teaching in the *Tipitaka* ("Three Baskets") ("The Major Systems," n.d., para. 1).

The Theravadins accept that there is an infinite number of cosmoses. Those cosmoses that are inhabited by people have three planes of existence: desire, material form, and immateriality. Each of the planes is further divided into various levels. For example, the plane of desire is divided into hell, the earth, and the heavens. Human existence is privileged.

"In this cosmos, as in all others, time moves in cycles of great duration involving a period of involution…a period of reformation of the cosmic structure, a series of cycles of decline and renewal, and finally, another period of involution from which the process is initiated once again" ("The Major Systems," n.d., para. 6).

One of the forms of meditation in the Theravada tradition involves four stages: "Closely related to a Hindu tradition of yoga, the first of these involves a process of moral and intellectual purification. Initially, the Theravadin meditator seeks to achieve detachment from sensual desires and impure states of mind through reflection and to enter a state of satisfaction and joy. In the second stage of this form of meditation, intellectual activity gives way to a complete inner serenity; the mind is in a state of 'one-pointedness' (concentration), joy, and pleasantness. In the third stage, every emotion, including joy, has disappeared, and the meditator is left indifferent to everything. In the fourth stage, satisfaction, any inclination to a good or bad state of mind, pain, and serenity are left behind, and the meditator enters a state of supreme purity, indifference, and pure consciousness" ("The Major Systems," n.d., para. 11).

Mahayana School. A second major branch of Buddhism is the Mahayana School. It also has many sub-branches, including the Avatamsaka School, the Madhyamika School, the Yogachara School, the Pure Land devotional schools, and many Meditation Schools.

For the Mahayanas, the self does not exist. The elite person is one who wants to be a Buddha and holds on entry into nirvana in order to help others. "In Bahayan, love for creatures is exalted to the highest" ("The Major Systems," n.d., para. 31). For the Mahayanas, Buddha is viewed as a supramundane being. He multiplies himself and is often reflected in other buddhas.

"As the tradition developed, there emerged new texts that were considered by Mahanyana adherents to be *Buddhavachana* ('the word or words of the Buddha'). This new literature went far beyond the ancient canons and was believed to be the highest revelation, superseding earlier texts. In this literature the teaching is thought to operate on various levels, each adapted to the intellectual capacity and karmic propensities of those who hear it" ("The Major Systems," n.d., para. 33).

In the Mahayana tradition there are two distinct categories of individuals: the enlightened and the unenlightened. The enlightened are able to understand more of the Buddha's teachings and reflect those teachings in their daily lives.

"The three bodies (*trikaya*; i.e., modes of being) of the Buddha are rooted in Hinayana teachings concerning the physical body, the mental body, and the body of the law. The theory of the three bodies was a subject of major discussion for the Mahayana, becoming part of the salvation process and assuming central significance in doctrine. The emanation body (*nirmanakaya*) is the form of the Buddha that appears in the world to teach people the path to liberation. The enjoyment (or bliss) body (*sambhogakaya*) is the celestial body of the Buddha to which contemplation can ascend. In the heavenly regions, or Pure Lands, the enjoyment body teaches the bodhisattva doctrines that are unintelligible to those who are unenlightened. The unmanifested body of the law (*dharmakaya*) already appears in the *Saddharmapundarika*, or *Lotus Sutra*, a transitional text of great importance to Mahayana devotional schools. In many Mahayana texts buddhas are infinite and share an identical nature – the *dharmakaya* ("The Major Systems," n.d., para. 36).

Pali Language

Pali is a Middle Indo-Aryan language originating in what is now India. The scriptures of Theravada Buddhism were originally written in Pali. "The Pali language is considered to be a composite language having several dialects and most likely is based on the language that Buddha taught in which is generally considered to be a Magadi dialect" (Prabhat, 2018, para. 4). Pali was spoken at least in the 1st century BCE. Pali is closely related to Sanskrit. However, "Pali is not considered to be a descendant of the Sanscrit language" (Prabhat, 2018, para 3).

Next we will consider how Buddhism and the cultural and social norms of the religion are revealed throughout business in an effort to prepare business professionals to effectively engage with Buddhists in the 21st century global business environment.

Buddhist Business Practices

Three principal doctrines of Buddhism provide the foundation for Buddhist business practices. The first is that human life involves suffering, the second is that the goal of life is to cease from suffering, and the third is that sufficiency is desirable. While Buddhists engage in economic development activity, they pursue it within the context of these core doctrines.

Thus the aim of Buddhist economic activities is the reduction of suffering instead of utility-and profit-maximization, and its possibility is confirmed by Prospect Theory. According to Prospect Theory, people are loss-sensitive. They are more sensitive to losses than gains, thus the minimization of losses could be a rational economic goal. The Buddhist economic paradigm is not merely different from the neoclassical economic paradigm, but exactly the opposite of that. It is based on bounded rationality, non-self, imperfect decision making, and aims at the reduction of suffering (Kovacs, 2014). This approach is in contrast to many other perspectives on business from around the world, whether religious or not.

Buddhist economic practice is distinguished by five characteristics:

> Minimize suffering – an economic enterprise is worthy if it aims to reduce the suffering for every stakeholder;

> Simplifying desires – rather than cultivating or multiplying desires, an economic enterprise should simplify desires, ensure contentment and encourage moderate consumption;

> Practicing non-violence – the reduction of violence to the lowest possible level is identical to the reduction of market forces to a small, adaptable scale for the benefit of every participant;

> Genuine care – the opposite of the instrumental use, treating stakeholders as goals not as tools in themselves; and

> Generosity – people are "home-reciprocants" as they tend to behave gratefully and reciprocate favors (Kovacs, 2014, p. 759).

Another way of talking about Buddhist economic activity is that its goal is to satisfy basic human needs while forsaking other consumer longings.

When business leaders apply these principles they must keep in mind that these goals and characteristics should also apply to all the stakeholders, especially the employees of the business. Employees are to be so situated that they can lead a balanced life, a life that allows for gainful work, but also spiritual development, and good family life. Employers must manage in such a way that the work is non-violent to the employees, other stakeholders, and to the general environment.

With these foundational principles in mind, we can move to other principles that should guide leaders as they direct businesses. Nine such principles are now articulated.

Employee Engagement

Leaders attempt to establish a culture of employee engagement. Research suggests that employee engagement is at the heart of a successful business. Engagement is found where work is absorbing, and to which employees feel naturally dedicated; work that one gets wrapped up in and is energized by. "Engaged employees are prepared to go beyond the call of duty and actually drive the business; they show up because they want to, not because they have to" (Beer & Gamble, 2017, para. 6).

As Buddhism has spread throughout the years, its philosophies and practices are subtly infused into the business environment in many areas of the world. In fact, many Buddhist philosophies have been translated into ten maxims for business. For example, the second Buddhist maxim for business states "None can live without toil, and a craft that provides your needs is a blessing indeed. But if you toil without rest, fatigue and weariness will overtake you, and you will [be] denied the joy that comes from labour's end" ("Ten Buddhist Maxims," n.d., para. 5).

Spiritual Goals

Buddhism does not negate commercial profit goals, but rather those goals must be considered in the context of spiritual goals as well. Finances must be considered in the context of meaning – where does money come from, how is it spent, how does the economic activity promote non-violence, social responsibility, and stakeholder enlightenment? What is the activity doing to enhance the quality of the larger society? All these must be taken into consideration to balance out the purely monetary goals that a firm must have.

Be Mindful

Buddhists believe that one should keep your head and heart calm, balanced, and objective. Do not let pride overtake you. One should not worry about positive or negative feedback. The third Buddhist maxim for business states "Develop the mind of equilibrium. You will always be getting praise and blame, but do not let either affect the poise of the mind: follow the calmness, the absence of pride" ("Ten Buddhist Maxims," n.d., para. 7).

Cause and Effect

Buddhists believe that every happening is caused by some previous activity. As the business leader sets goals he or she must determine what will be the causes that lead to the realization of that goal. "The process is like reverse engineering. We start to trace back the logical sequence of actions that would lead to a defined goal. This process helps to define the needed steps to achieve the goal and forms a good basis for a road map for the project" (Milyutin, n.d., para. 5).

One Step at a Time

As the firm moves toward meeting its economic and spiritual goals, it does not need to rush to the end. Take it one step at a time using appropriate Buddhist principles. For example, the tenth Buddhist maxim for business states "A jug fills drop by drop. This classic saying from the Buddha means that things happen step by step, and that methodological piecemeal work is often superior to big splashes" ("Ten Buddhist Maxims," n.d., para. 13).

Solve a Customer's Problem

Businesses will be successful if they discover customers' problems and help those customers resolve those problem. "So, understanding a problem our potential customers might be facing and having an empathetic attitude toward it are crucial" (Milyutin, n.d., para. 8). A customer's problem causes the customer to suffer, and businesses that help customers solve problems are views as compassionate. "Compassion is the wish for others to be rid of their sufferings" (Milyutin, n.d., para. 7).

Embrace Change

Reality involves change. Everything around us, including ourselves, is changing. The government, the environment, the people, our jobs, our families. We should not become fixated on a particular concept or physical object and expect it to remain changeless over time. We must embrace change, and be prepared to act in the context of the changed environment (Milyutin, n.d.).

While embracing change, we should not get wrapped up in mourning for the past or yearning for the future. Buddhist maxim number eight declares "Do not dwell in the past, do not dream of the future, concentrate the mind on the present moment" ("Ten Buddhist Maxims," n.d., para. 10). This perspective demonstrates a commitment to acceptance of change without at the same time negating the realism of current existence. The ninth Buddhist maxim for business states "You can only lose what you cling to" ("Ten Buddhist Maxims," n.d., para. 11). The Buddha's teachings are clear on this – everything is in a constant state of change, and nothing is permanent. Therefore, they key to happiness is to maintain flexibility, adaptability, and a sincere desire to accept what comes as to avoid disappointment ("Ten Buddhist Maxims," n.d.).

Do Good to All

We must help guide our fellow humans from around the globe to move in the right direction of alleviating suffering and providing a good life for all. Not only must we think good thoughts about helpful activities, we must also, each one of us, act on those good thoughts. According to Buddhist maxim for business number seven, "Every individual has a responsibility to help guide our global family in the right direction. Good wishes are not sufficient; we must become actively engaged" ("Ten Buddhist Maxims," n.d., para. 9).

To carry this out we must be mindful of the world around us. As Buddhist maxim for business number six states, "Your work is to discover your world and then with all your heart give yourself to it" ("Ten Buddhist Maxims," n.d., para. 7).

Sufficiency is Acceptable and Reasonable

Much has been written about the Buddhist's view on business and economics. Schumacher (1973), as cited by Ashtankar (2015), gave pointers about Buddhist economics. "He said that Buddhist economics is a 'Middle way' of development, aiming to achieve maximum well-being with minimum consumption" (Ashtankar, 2015, p. 17). Therefore, business professionals should not procure lavish belongings or live a life of material abundance.

In alignment with corporate social responsibility ideas of the West, Buddhists believe that personal interests should not be one's first or only pursuit. Buddhists believe that each individual has a responsibility to one another, society, and nature, and must consider the needs of these in conjunction with their lifestyle (Ashtankar, 2015).

Thus profit maximization should not be the goal of our business. Rather, we must have profits that will help us meet our basic necessities of life and ameliorate the sufferings of our customers. We must all strive to follow the Eightfold Path (Ashtankar, 2015).

Doing Business in Thailand

The country with the highest percentage of Buddhists is Thailand, with approximately 64% of the 68 million total population subscribing to Buddhism. Given the pervasive influence of Buddhism throughout the country, Thailand was selected as the best representation of the convergence of Buddhism with business practices.

Thailand is located in Southeast Asia, with neighboring countries being Laos, Cambodia, Myanmar, and Malaysia. In land mass it is approximately three times the size of the State of Florida in the United States.

The country, established in the mid-1200s (1238), was formerly known as Siam until just before World War II. In the 1930s there was a revolution which led to a constitutional monarchy. The Japanese invaded Thailand in 1941. After World War II the country became an ally of the United States. In the last half of the 20th century the country underwent several coups of a military or civilian nature which eventually led to a new constitution which was adopted in 2017. King Phumiphon, after being on the throne for 70 years, died in 2016; his son, Washiralongkon, became King later that year.

About 40% of the land is agricultural. Forty-nine percent of the population is urbanized, with approximately 10 million people in or near Bangkok, the nation's capital. Natural resources include natural gas, rubber, tin, lead, and gypsum (Central Intelligence Agency, 2018e).

Life expectancy at birth in 74.9 years. Of the population age 15 and older, 92.9% are literate (Central Intelligence Agency, 2018e).

The legal system used in Thailand is based on civil law. Head of state is King Washiralongkon; the monarchy is hereditary. The head of government is the

Prime Minister. The new constitution calls for a bicameral parliament, with 250 members in a Senate and 500 members in a House of Representatives. The next elections are expected in 2019. The judicial branch consists of a Supreme Court of Justice, a Constitutional Court, and a Supreme Administrative Court (Central Intelligence Agency, 2018e).

Thailand is a member of the United Nations, the International Monetary Fund, and the World Trade Organization. "Thailand's economic fundamentals are sound, with low inflation, low unemployment, and reasonable public and external debt levels" (Central Intelligence Agency, 2018e, p. 5). GDP for 2017 was $1.234 trillion in Purchase Power Parity. At official exchange rates the 2017 GDP estimate was $455.4 billion. The 2017 real growth rate of the GDP was estimated at 3.9%. Per capita GDP for 2017 was estimated at $17,990 at Purchase Power Parity. The percentage of the population below the poverty line was estimated at 7.2% in 2015 (Central Intelligence Agency, 2018e).

There have been ongoing problems for some time along the Malaysia border with separatist groups in the predominantly Malay-Muslim provinces. Thailand has been a center of human trafficking for years, and there is a problem with drug usage and drug transportation in the country.

Foreign direct investment in Thailand is welcomed. The government has several incentive programs to reduce taxation for foreign entities investing in Thailand. Special incentives are available for firms placing their international headquarters in Thailand (Central Intelligence Agency, 2018e).

Various types of legal organizations are available in Thailand. Included are partnerships, joint ventures, unincorporated joint ventures, private limited companies, public limited companies, and branch offices of foreign companies.

The currency of Thailand is the Thai Baht. At the time of this writing the exchange rate with the U.S. dollar was $1=32.2156 Bahts. Foreign currencies can be brought into and removed from Thailand (Central Intelligence Agency, 2018e).

Electrification of the county is estimated at 99%. Subscriptions to fixed-line telephones number 2.91 million and subscriptions to cellular phones is 121.53 million. Internet users are estimated at 32 million (Central Intelligence Agency, 2018e).

The official language of Thailand is Thai. English is the second most spoken language. Foreigners desiring to enter Thailand must obtain a visa. The type of visa depends on the expected stay of the foreigner in Thailand. Visa holders must report to the Department of Immigration every 90 days. Foreigners working in Thailand must have work permits, with some exceptions (Central Intelligence Agency, 2018e).

Thailand attempts to protect intellectual property. Copyrights may be obtained which protect information during the creator's life and 50 years after the creator's death. Patents for inventions hold for 20 years and patents for designs hold for 10 years. Trademarks may be registered (Central Intelligence Agency, 2018e).

Foreign companies doing business in Thailand and domestic companies pay corporate income taxes. The tax system is progressive with the highest rates set at 20%. Individuals pay personal income tax with rates up to 35%. A Value Added Tax (VAT) of 7% applies to many business transactions (Central Intelligence Agency, 2018e).

Thirteen holidays are observed by government offices and most businesses. They are:

1 January	New Year's Day
February, 3rd week	Makha Bucha Day
6 April	Chakri Memorial Day
13-15 April	Songkran
5 May	Coronation Day
13-15 May	National Labour Day
May, 3rd week	Visakha Bucha Day
July, 3rd week	Asarnha Bucha Day
12 August	H. M. The Queen's Birthday
23 October	Chulalongkorn Memorial Day
5 December	The King's Birthday
10 December	Constitution Day
1 December	New Year's Eve Day

Buddhism

The state religion of Thailand is Theravada Buddhism. "One cannot deny the fact that in the Thai society, Buddhism has long borne much influence over the Thai way of life, thoughts and behavior. Further, Buddhism has been the main driving force in the Thai cultural development" (Limanonda, 1995, p. 77). There are over 30,000 Buddhist temples, over 300,000 monks and more than 100,000 novices. "The application of the Dhamma, the Buddha's principles, is vast in all kinds of organizations in the society" (p. 68).

A specific aspect of Buddhism that is practiced in Thailand is the principle of hierarchical order. "The vertical social relationship is characterized by a formalized superordinate-subordinate relationship" (Limanonda, 1995, p. 69). The King is considered to be the patron of religion. "You are subordinate to the old, women are subordinate to men, layman (sic) are subordinate to monks, and the villagers are subordinate to the headman" (p. 69).

The locus of introduction into the culture is found in the family. The family is to be an exemplar of the hierarchical order, and the children are to be indoctrinated into that value system in the family setting.

Although the macro culture is collectivist, individual initiative and action is prized. It is viewed that this is an outcome of Theravada Buddhism with its emphasis on individual initiative and tolerance (Limanonda, 1995).

Cultural Practices

Harmony, patience, and personal equilibrium are prized values in Thailand. Do not be loud or boisterous. Being calm in one's demeanor is prized. Being publicly angry will result in loss of face.

Remember that Thailand is the land of *mai pen rai*, which means "it doesn't matter." Difficulties are to be ignored as much as possible. Even a death in the family should be taken with detachment. An attitude of fatalism is expected.

Thailand is the Land of Smiles. Smiling, but not giggling, is acceptable and desired. Smiling can be used to cover embarrassment and to apologize for mistakes.

Good face is very important in Thailand. Do not say or do anything that would cause another person or yourself to lose face. Loss of face in a business venture may well close down communication between principals with a subsequent loss of the venture.

Thailand is a collectivist society with much emphasis on hierarchy, seniority and age. Most business decisions are made at the top of the organization. A business professional should know where any counterpart stands in his or her organization; expect those low in an organization to pass decision-making to people higher up in the system.

When meeting another person, the traditional greeting is the *wai*, which is a gesture of bringing the palms together in front of the chest, with fingers pointing up, and a slight bow. People of high status are given a *wai* with the hands higher on the chest. If a handshake is offered, then go ahead and shake hands.

Business cards should be used. It is good practice to have the information given in Thai on one side of the card and English on the other. Business cards should be presented and received with both hands. A received business card should be accepted respectfully and handled carefully; do not put the business card in a back pocket.

Be very careful with shoes and their use. It is customary to remove shoes when entering a house. Do not show the soles of the shoe to another person, since the shoe is the dirtiest part of a person's clothes. Do not point the toes at another person, for the evil spirits in the shoe may attack the other person.

Do not cross your legs with one leg placed on the other knee. Don't touch another person's head or back. Be careful to give rite of passage to monks and to the elderly.

Thailand has a relationship society. People wanting to do business should establish a relationship with a key person in the partnering company, then develop and maintain the relationship over time. Developing the relationship may take several meetings and trips between the two person's offices and homes. The relationship between the two companies will be personalized in the people who work together. If the personnel change, the incoming replacement personnel will need to build a new relationship.

Contracts are typically shorter than would be the case between two western companies. Contracts contain the beginnings of the working relationship. It is realized that difficulties may come later, but because of the good relationships between the principal parties those difficulties will be resolved.

Be on time for business meetings; punctuality is appreciated. Be careful to allow plenty of time to get to the meeting if it is in Bangkok, since traffic there is notoriously bad. In going to a meeting, it is better not to go in cold. Rather, have a third party introduce you or have a letter of introduction from someone who knows the party you are visiting.

Address people by their title and surname. For example, if you are meeting with an engineer whose surname is Hu, address him as Engineer Hu. As always, be very respectful of names.

Finally, never say anything negative about the King or any member of the royal family.

Truth, Negotiations, and Values

Truth comes from the Middle Way, that is, it comes from understanding both sides of a situation. "The truth develops from subjective, fatalistic feelings on the issue modified by faith in the ideologies of Theravada Buddhism" (Morrison & Conaway, 2006, p. 509). Thais welcome information that will help them make decisions. However, people and families take precedence over the abstract law. "The individual is responsible for his or her decisions" (Morrison & Conaway, 2006, p. 509).

"Decision-making revolves around the hierarchical, centralized nature of authority and the dependence of the subordinate upon the superior" (Morrison & Conaway, 2006, p. 509).

As suggested above, face is extremely important. Status comes from karma, not one's personal success (Morrison & Conaway, 2006). In negotiations do not force your counterpart to give you a "yes" or "no" answer. Thais will not want to give a no answer because it may interrupt harmony and cause the respondent to lose face. Do not confront the person with whom you are negotiating.

Conclusion

In conclusion, the 21st century global business environment is more geographically and culturally diverse than at any time in history. This phenomenon will only continue going forward, as more and more countries join the global business community. As such, business professionals throughout the world must be prepared to effectively navigate the cultural and religious labyrinth that is an integral part of our current business reality. Understanding how religious customs and rituals impact business in countries that are strongly influenced by religious tradition is paramount for business professionals to be successful.

This page intentionally left blank

CHAPTER 5
WORKING IN RELIGIOUS CULTURES

Readers of the previous four chapters now have a basic understanding of four major world religions and their impact on the practice of business. The number of adherents of the four religions considered — Islam, Judaism, Hinduism and Buddhism — is approximately four billion people. Adding in the adherents of Christianity, we get to six billion people, or two-thirds of the world's population.

Business professionals working internationally need to understand the cultures in which they are working. Global business research shows that one of the principal reasons global businesses collapse is because of failure to understand and appreciate the cultures in which they operate. Here culture involves such matters as world view, ethics, perspectives on life's priorities, legal systems, relationship to material goods, importance of interpersonal relationships, religion, and many other facets of culture.

It is apparent that religious teachings and beliefs interact strongly with the individual, family, and aggregate cultures in which people live. One cannot fully understand another person until one knows what that person believes about religious matters. Does that person accept, believe, and live the religion dominant in that person's environment? If not, why not? If the person does believe in the dominant religion, does that belief translate into action congruent with those religious beliefs?

Most of the readers of this book live in a society where Christianity is the dominant religion and heritage. Also, most readers live in Northern America or Northern Europe, regions of individualist cultures. Christianity and individualism shape the reader's culture, and influence thinking and action in business practices.

With Christian and individualist principles as a foundation for world view, readers will be able to contrast and compare each of the four other religions to their own world views. There follows some commentary on the relationships between Christian/individualist perspectives and the other four religions.

The most difference between two cultures is found between Islamic business practices and standard U.S. and European practices. Arguably the most important differing elements of Islamic finance are the prohibitions against riba and gharar. Another significant difference is the personal practices observant Muslims have in their daily lives. Otherwise, business practices in terms of honesty, strong relationships, and good human resource management practices would be similar to those in Northern America and Northern Europe.

Business practices of Jews are quite similar to and compatible with business practice in Northern America and Northern Europe. For example, a worker moving from Canada to Israel would not find much difference between a company in Canada and one in Israel. Human resource management practices would be similar. Unless the person is working for an Orthodox

Jew in Israel, demands on personal life activities would be minimal, just like they would be in Canada.

Hindu and Buddhist business practices would be similar to those in the United States. However, the pace may be slower, and the attitudes of the workers may be different with respect to the acquisition of material goods. The Buddhist doctrine of sufficiency is considerably different from attitudes toward material acquisition typical of people in Northern America and Northern Europe. Also, the development of good and lasting relationships are more important in Hindu and Buddhist business practice. Further, the working situation with respect to the boss will ascribe more authority to the boss and less independence to the worker.

This page intentionally left blank

REFERENCES

AAOIFI. (n.d.). Accounting and Auditing Organization for Islamic Financial Institutions. Retrieved May 14, 2019 from http://aaoifi.com/about-aaoifi/?lang=en

A list of the 613 Mitzvot (Commandments). (n.d.). *Judaism 101.* Retrieved from http://www.jewfaq.org/613.htm

Aich, D., & Mathias, S. (2018, December 12). Employment & labour law in India. *Lexology.* Retrieved from https://www.lexology.com/library/detail.aspx?g=fa2f b547-5828-419a-bd3b-4ef01b612643

Al-Qazwini, S.M. (n.d.). Invitation to Islam. *Ahlul Bayt Digital Islamic Library Project.* Retrieved April 24, 2008 from http://al-islam.org/invitation/toc.htm

Ali, A.J., Gibbs, M., & Camp, R.C. (2000). Human resource strategy: The Ten Commandments perspective. *International Journal of Sociology and Social Policy, 20*(5/6), 114-132.

Amin, H. (n.d.). The origins of the Sunni/Shia split in Islam. *Islam for Today.* Retrieved April 28, 2008 from http://www.islamfortoday.com/shia.htm

An Asian religion gains popularity in the New World. (2018, April 13). *The Economist.* Retrieved from https://www.economist.com/erasmus/2018/04/13/a n-asian-religion-gains-popularity-in-the-new-world

Armstrong, K. (2002). *Islam: A short history*. New York: Random House

Ashtankar, O.M. (2015). Relevance of Buddhism for business management. *International Journal of Applied Research*, *1*(13), 17-20. Retrieved from http://www.allresearchjournal.com/archives/2015/vol1issue13/PartA/1-13-4.pdf

As-Siba'i, M. (n.d.). Introduction to the Sunnah and its position in the Islamic law. *Islam Online Archive*. Retrieved May 27, 2019 from http://www.islam.com/Article.aspx?id=240

Babur: The founder of the empire which ruled India for over 300 years. (2016, December 26). India Today. Retrieved from https://www.indiatoday.in/education-today/gk-current-affairs/story/mughal-emperor-babur-839094-2016-12-26

Bazian, A.R. (2018, December 16). Islamic microfinance sector moves towards consumer-friendly debt instruments with borrower welfare in mind. *Jordan Times*. Retrieved from https://jordantimes.com/news/local/islamic-microfinance-sector-moves-towards-consumer-friendly-debt-instruments-borrower

Beer, H., & Gamble, E. (2017, October 2). What business can learn from Buddhism. *The Conversation*. University of Warwick. Retrieved from https://theconversation.com/what-business-can-learn-from-buddhism-84413

Bennett, S.N., Guillen, S., Nelson, T., Olsen, S., Smart, C., & Waller, A. (2010). Transcultural nursing: Hindu culture. *Utah Valley University*. Retrieved from http://freebooks.uvu.edu/NURS3400/index.php/ch1 3-hindu-culture.html

Birnbaum, Y. (2016, October 21). Torah's take on sexual abuse. *The Jewish Chronicle*. Retrieved from https://www.thejc.com/comment/comment/torah-s-take-on-sexual-abuse-1.54243

Brahman. (n.d.). In *The Yogic Encyclopedia*. Retrieved May 16, 2019 from https://www.ananda.org/yogapedia/brahman/

B'rit Milah: The circumcision ritual. (n.d.). *ReformJudaism.org*. Retrieved May 15, 2019 from https://reformjudaism.org/brit-milah-circumcision-ritual

Buddhism: Basic beliefs. (n.d.). *United Religions Initiative*. Retrieved May 17, 2019 from https://www.uri.org/kids/world-religions/buddhist-beliefs

Buddhism. (2018, August 23). *History.com* Retrieved from https://www.history.com/topics/religion/buddhism #section_3

Buddhism. (2019). In *Encyclopedia Britannica Online*. Retrieved May 17, 2019 from https://www.britannica.com/topic/Buddhism

Buddhists. (2019). *Pew Research Center*. Retrieved May 17, 2019 from http://www.pewforum.org/religious-landscape-study/religious-tradition/buddhist/

Business and ethics. (2016, April 21). *The Hindu Business Line*. Retrieved from https://www.thehindubusinessline.com/opinion/editorial/ethics-and-business/article21476376.ece

Carr, K.E. (2017, July 22). Science and math in ancient India. *Quatr.us Study Guides*. Retrieved from https://quatr.us/india/science-math-ancient-india.htm

Carson, E. (2018, May 1). Attire for women traveling in India for business. *USA Today*. Retrieved from https://traveltips.usatoday.com/attire-women-traveling-india-business-60024.html

Castro, J. (2013, November 22). What is karma? *Live Science*. Retrieved from https://www.livescience.com/41462-what-is-karma.html

Central Intelligence Agency. (2018). *The World Factbook*. Retrieved May 16, 2019 from https://www.cia.gov/library/publications/the-world-factbook/

Central Intelligence Agency. (2018a). Egypt. In *The World Factbook*. Retrieved May 16, 2019 from https://www.cia.gov/library/publications/the-world-factbook/geos/eg.html

Central Intelligence Agency. (2018b). India. In *The World Factbook*. Retrieved May 16, 2019 from https://www.cia.gov/library/publications/the-world-factbook/geos/in.html

Central Intelligence Agency. (2018c). Mauritius. In *The World Factbook*. Retrieved May 16, 2019 from https://www.cia.gov/library/publications/the-world-factbook/geos/mp.html

Central Intelligence Agency (2018d). Nepal. In *The World Factbook*. Retrieved May 16, 2019 from https://www.cia.gov/library/publications/the-world-factbook/geos/np.html

Central Intelligence Agency (2018e). Thailand. In *The World Factbook*. Retrieved May 16, 2019 from https://www.cia.gov/library/publications/the-world-factbook/geos/th.html

Chatterjee, P. (2017, November 25). Breaking trends: Indian women now prefer western wear. *The Hindu Business Line*. Retrieved from https://www.thehindubusinessline.com/news/Breaking-trends-Indian-women-now-prefer-western-wear/article20763360.ece

Chattopadhyay, C. (2012). Indian philosophy and business ethics: A review. *Advances in Management and Applied Economics, 2*(3), 111-123.

Choate, A. (2013, November 8). Why do Hindus wear turbans? *The White Hindu*. Retrieved from http://www.patheos.com/blogs/whitehindu/2013/11

/why-do-hindus-wear-turbans-google-questions-answered/

Chronology. (n.d.). *University of Southern California.* Retrieved April 30, 2008 from http://www.usc.edu/dept/MSA/history/chronology/century6.html

Country comparison. (n.d.). *Hofstede Insights.* Retrieved May 15, 2019 from https://www.hofstede-insights.com/country-comparison/israel/

Cragg, K. (1969). *The house of Islam.* Belmont, CA: Dickenson.

Das, S. (2018, August 10). The 4 stages of life in Hinduism. *Learn Religions.* Retrieved from https://www.learnreligions.com/stages-of-life-in-hinduism-1770068

Dawood, N.J. (1974). *The Koran.* New York: Penguin Books.

Demographics of Buddhism. (n.d.). *Georgetown University Berkley Center for Religion, Peace, & World Affairs.* Retrieved May 27, 2019 from https://berkleycenter.georgetown.edu/essays/demographics-of-buddhism

Devon Bank. (n.d.). Retrieved May 15, 2019 from http://www.devonbank.com/Islamic

Doing business in Egypt. (2016). *Grant Thornton / HSBC.* Retrieved from https://www.business.hsbc.ca/-/media/library/markets/egypt/pdf/egypt-final.pdf

Doing business in Egypt. (n.d.). *Today Translations.* Retrieved May 27, 2019 from https://www.todaytranslations.com/doing-business-in-egypt.

Dowdey, S. (n.d.). How reincarnation works. *HowStuffWorks.* Retrieved May 27, 2019 from https://people.howstuffworks.com/reincarnation2.htm

Dunn, S.L., & Galloway, R.R. (2011, November). Islam, Islamic finance, and Christianity. *Journal of Biblical Integration in Business, 14*(1), 43-67.

Dunn, S.L., & Jensen, J.D. (2018, July). Judaism and Jewish business practices. International *Journal of Business Administration, 9*(4), 73-88.

Dunn, S.L., & Jensen, J.D. (2019a). Hinduism and Hindu business practices. International *Journal of Business Administration, 10*(1), 33-48.

Dunn, S.L., & Jensen, J.D. (2019b). Buddhism and Buddhist business practices. *International Journal of Business Administration, 10*(2), 115-128.

East India Company and Raj 1785-1858. (n.d.). *Parliament.uk.* Retrieved May 16, 2019 from https://www.parliament.uk/about/living-heritage/evolutionofparliament/legislativescrutiny/parliament-and-empire/parliament-and-the-american-colonies-before-1765/east-india-company-and-raj-1785-1858/

Ebrahim, S.M. (2011, September). Islamic banking in Sudan. Retrieved from https://www.researchgate.net/publication/228202433 _Islamic_Banking_in_Sudan

El-Gamal, M.A. (2006). *Islamic finance: Law, economics, and practice.* New York: Cambridge.

Four denominations of Hinduism. (2003). *Hinduism Today Magazine.* Retrieved from https://www.hinduismtoday.com/modules/smartsect ion/item.php?itemid=3784

Four stages of life. (n.d.). Hinduism facts: Facts about Hindu religion. Retrieved May 16, 2019 from http://www.hinduismfacts.org/four-stages-of-life/

Friedman, H.H. (2001). The impact of Jewish values on marketing and business practices. *Journal of Macromarketing, 21*(1), 74-80. Retrieved from https://doi.org/10.1177/0276146701211007

Gannon, J. (2017, December 30). The ten spiritual realms: According to an ancient Japanese Buddhist priest from the Kamakura period. *Collective Evolution.* Retrieved from https://www.collective-evolution.com/2017/12/30/the-ten-spiritual-realms-according-to-an-ancient-japanese-buddhist-priest-from-the-kamakura-period/

Gosal, D. (2013, April 24). History of economic growth in India. *International Policy Digest.* Retrieved from https://intpolicydigest.org/20130/04/24/history-of-economic-growth-in-india

Gradinaru, A., & Iavorschi, M. (2013). The Hindu economic system. *Human and Social Studies*, 2(2). doi:10.2478/hssr-2013-0003

Gundogdu, A.S. (2018). The rise of Islamic finance: 2-step murabaha. *Asia-Pacific Management Accounting Journal*, 13(1), 107-130. Retrieved from https://www.researchgate.net/publication/329584948_THE_RISE_OF_ISLAMIC_FINANCE_2-STEP_MURABAHA

Head, G. (2006). Where our ethics come from. *International Risk Management Institute*. Retrieved from https://www.irmi.com/articles/expert-commentary/where-our-ethics-come-from

Herman, J.E. (n.d.). Everything you need to know about Shabbat services. *RerformJudaism.org*. Retrieved May 16, 2019 from https://reformjudaism.org/jewish-holidays/shabbat/everything-you-need-know-about-shabbat-services

Hesselink, K. (n.d.). History of Buddha and Buddhism. Retrieved May 17, 2019 from http://www.katinkahesselink.net/tibet/his.html

Hindu beliefs. (2016, November 18). *ReligionFacts*. Retrieved from http://www.religionfacts.com/hinduism/beliefs

Hindu history. (2016, November 18). *ReligionFacts*. Retrieved from http://www.religionfacts.com/hinduism/history

Hindu holidays in 2019. (n.d.). *Timebie*. Retrieved May 16, 2019 from http://www.timebie.com/calendar/hindu2019.php

Hindu law. (2017, December 24). In *New World Encyclopedia*. Retrieved from https://www.newworldencyclopedia.org/entry/Hindu_Law

Hinduism. (2018, August 23). *History.com*. Retrieved from https://www.history.com/topics/religion/hinduism

Hinduism by country. (n.d.). In *Wikipedia*. Retrieved May 16, 2019 from https://en.wikipedia.org/wiki/Hinduism_by_country

Hofstede, G., Hofstede, G.J., & Minkov, M. (2010). *Cultures and organizations: Software of the mind*. New York: McGraw Hill.

Index of anti-Semitism. (2015). *ADL Global 100*. Retrieved from http://global100.adl.org/#map/country

Iqbal, Z., & Mirakhor, A. (2007). *An introduction to Islamic finance: Theory and practice*. Singapore: Wiley.

Islamic banking operating model. (2017, May 13). *Islamic Bankers Resource Centre*. Retrieved from https://islamicbankers.me/tag/islamic-banking-windows/

Islamic history (Chronology). (n.d.). *Barkati.net.* Retrieved May 24, 2019 from http://www.barkati.net/english/chronology.htm

Iverson, K. (2017a, October 27). Everything you need to know about Buddhism in Thailand. *The Culture Trip.* Retrieved from https://theculturetrip.com/asia/thailand/articles/everything-you-need-to-know-about-buddhism-in-thailand/

Iverson, K. (2017b, March 9). An etiquette guide to visiting temples in Thailand. *The Culture Trip.* Retrieved from https://theculturetrip.com/asia/thailand/articles/an-etiquette-guide-to-visiting-temples-in-thailand/

Jacobs, J. (n.d.). Ethical treatment of animals in Judaism. *My Jewish Learning.* Retrieved May 16, 2019 from http://www.myjewishlearning.com/article/ethical-treatment-of-animals-in-judaism

Jamaldeen, F. (n.d.). The mudaraba contract in Islamic finance. Retrieved May 16, 2019 from https://www.dummies.com/personal-finance/islamic-finance/the-mudaraba-contract-in-islamic-finance/

Jayaram V. (n.d.-a). The Buddha on God. Retrieved from May 17, 2019 from https://www.hinduwebsite.com/Buddhism/buddhaongod.asp

Jayaram V. (n.d.-b). Hinduism concepts, beliefs and practices. *Hinduwebsite.com*. Retrieved May 16, 2019 from http://www.hinduwebsite.com/hinduism.asp

Jayaram V. (n.d.-c). The diversity and the plurality of Hinduism. *Hinduwebsite.com*. Retrieved May 16, 2019 from https://www.hinduwebsite.com/hinduintrod5.asp

Jordan, M. (2002). *Islam: An illustrated history*. London: Carlton.

Katz, L. (2011). Negotiating international business: The negotiator's reference guide to 50 countries around the world. *Amazon Digital Services*.

Kaul, C. (2011, March 3). From empire to independence: The British Raj in India 1858-1947. Retrieved from http://www.bbc.co.uk/history/british/modern/indep endence1947_01.shtml

Kettell, B. (2010). *Islamic finance in a nutshell*. West Sussex, UK: Wiley.

Kohler, K. (2015). Jewish theology: Systematically and historically considered. New York: Andesite.

Kovacs, G. (2014). The theoretical foundation of Buddhist management practices. *Journal of Management Development*, 33(8/9), 751-762. Retrieved from https://doi.org/10.1108/JMD-09-2013-0120

Kuran, T. (2018). Islam and economic performance: Historical and contemporary links. *Journal of Economic*

Literature, 56(4), 1292-1359. Retrieved from https://doi.org/10.1257/jel.20171243

Lee, M. (2016, May 1). Ten worlds – Ten spiritual realms in Buddhist cosmology. *Lotus Happiness.* Retrieved from https://www.lotus-happiness.com/ten-worlds-ten-spiritual-realms-in-buddhist-cosmology/

Limanonda, B. (1995). Families in Thailand: Beliefs and realities. *Journal of Comparative Family Studies, 26*(1), 67-82. Retrieved from http://www.jstor.org/stable/41602367

Lodahl, M. (2010). *Claiming Abraham: Reading the Bible and the Qur'an side by side.* Grand Rapids, MI: Brazos.

Maternity leave & paternity leave benefits in India. (n.d.). *Helpline Law.* Retrieved May 16, 2019 from http://www.helplinelaw.com/family-law/MPBI1/maternity-leave-and-paternity-leavebenefits-in-india.html

Mashiach: The Messiah. (n.d.). *Judaism 101.* Retrieved May 16, 2019 from http://www.jewfaq.org/mashiach.htm

Meaning of life (Hinduism). (2016, November 19). *ReligionFacts.* Retrieved from http://www.religionfacts.com/hinduism/meaning-life

Medieval sourcebook: From the Sunnah. (n.d.). *Fordham University.* Retrieved May 10, 2019 from http://www.fordham.edu/halsall/source/sunnah-horne.html

Meir, A. (1996). Value conflicts in Jewish business ethics: Social versus fiduciary responsibility. *Jewish Law*. Retrieved from https://www.jlaw.com/Articles/fiduciary.html

Merryman, L. (2018, April 27). The story and spread of Buddhism. *International Mission Board*. Retrieved from https://www.imb.org/2018/04/27/story-spread-buddhism/

Messianic. (n.d.). What is Messianic Judaism? Retrieved May 16, 2019 from https://www.gotquestions.org/Messianic-Judaism.html

Miles, J. (2018). *God in the Qur'an*. New York: Knopf.

Milyutin, Y. (n.d.). 5 Buddhist principles to help run a business. *Study Buddhism*. Retrieved May 27, 2019 from https://studybuddhism.com/en/essentials/how-to/5-buddhist-principles-to-help-run-a-business

Mohamed, H.H., Masih, M., & Bacha, O.I. (2015, September). Why do issuers issue Sukuk or conventional bond? Evidence from Malaysian listed firms using partial adjustment models. *Pacific-Basin Finance Journal, 34*, 233-252. Retrieved from https://doi.org/10.1016/j.pacfin.2015.02.004

Morrison, T., & Conway, W.A. (2006). *Kiss, bow, or shake hands: The bestselling guide to doing business in more than 60 countries* (2nd ed.). Avon, MA: Adams Media.

Mukherjee, R. (2017, May 30). Work-life balance key driver of employee retention. *The Hindu*. Retrieved from https://www.thehindu.com/education/careers/work-life-balance-key-driver-of-employee-retention/article18589791.ece

Murphy, D. (2007, January 17). Islam's Sunni-Shiite split: A look at the historic divide within the Muslim world. Christian Science Monitor. Retrieved from http://www.csmonitor.com/2007/0117/p25s01-wome.html

Nain, V. (2018). Second urbanization in the chronology of Indian history. *International Journal of Academic Research and Development, 3*(2), 538-542.

Nasr, S.H. (2003). *Islam: Religion, history, and civilization.* New York: Harper Collins.

Natesan, N.C., Keeffe, M.J., & Darling, J.R. (2009). Enhancement of global business practices: Lessons from the Hindu Bhagavce Gita. *European Business Review, 21*(2), 128-143. Retrieved from https://www.emeraldinsight.com/doi/abs/10.1108/09555340910940132

Nation of Islam. (n.d.). *NOI.org.* Retrieved May 16, 2008 from http://www.noi.org

New data: 63 percent of global SMBS report international business growth. (2017, May 4). *Global Trade.* Retrieved from http://www.globaltrademag.com/global-logistics/new-data-63-percent-global-smbs-report-international-business-growth

Nine basic Hindu beliefs. (2009). *Hinduism Today Magazine*. Retrieved from https://www.hinduismtoday.com/modules/smartsect ion/item.php?itemid=3106

O'Brien, B. (2018, July 28). About Buddhist monks. *Learn Religions*. Retrieved from https://www.learnreligions.com/about-buddhist-monks-449758

O'Brien, B. (2019, January 15). Rebirth and reincarnation in Buddhism. *Learn Religions*. Retrieved from https://www.learnreligions.com/reincarnation-in-buddhism-449994

O'Donnell, R. (2018, April 3). Managers say they lack training, and 44% feel overwhelmed at work. *HR Drive*. Retrieved from https://www.hrdive.com/news/managers-say-they-lack-training-and-44-feel-overwhelmed-at-work/520396/

O'Neill, D. (2008). Next step in Islamic finance: Build a regulatory framework. *Euromoney, 39*(466),122-123. Retrieved from https://www.euromoney.com/article/b13229dvjtzq2d /next-step-in-islamic-finance-build-a-regulatory-framework

Orthodox Jewish population rising in U.S. (2016). *Hidabroot*. Retrieved from https://www.hidabroot.com/article/192393/Orthodo x-Jewish-Population-Rising-in-US

Ozdincer, B., & Yuce, Q.A. (2018). Stakeholder returns of Islamic banks versus conventional banks. *Emerging Markets Finance and Trade, 54*(14), 3330-3350. Retrieved from https://doi.org/10.1080/1540496X.2017.1393746

Pal, S. (2016, July 30). 16 significant science and tech discoveries ancient India gave the world. *The Better India.* Retrieved from https://www.thebetterindia.com/63119/ancient-india-science-technology/

Perry, M.S. (1993). *Jewish Labor Committee.* Retrieved from http://www.jewishlaborcommittee.org/LaborRightsIn TheJewishtradition.pdf

Pew Research Center. (2007, May 22). Muslim Americans: Middle class and mostly mainstream. Retrieved from http://www.nubank.com/islamic/muslim_americans. pdf

Platt, G. (2007, November 1). Shariah-compliant corporate finance forges ahead. *Global Finance.* Retrieved from https://www.gfmag.com/magazine/november-2007/di281f-features

Pollard, J.F. (2008). *Money and the rise of the modern papacy: Financing the Vatican, 1850-1950.* Cambridge: Cambridge University Press.

Prabhat, S. (2018, January 9). Difference between Sanskrit and Pali. *DifferenceBetween.net.* Retrieved from http://www.differencebetween.net/miscellaneous/culture-miscellaneous/difference-between-sanskrit-and-pali/

Public holidays in Egypt. (2019). *Office Holidays*. Retrieved from https://www.officeholidays.com/countries/egypt/index.php

Qurabn, S., & Alansari, M. (2017, June 15). Islamic credit cards — An introduction. Retrieved from https://ifinanceexpert.wordpress.com/2017/06/15/islamic-credit-cards-an-introduction/

Rahim, M. H. (n.d.). An introduction to Islam. *Ahlul Bayt Digital Islamic Library Project*. Retrieved April 24, 2008 from http://al-islam.org/begin/intro/rahim.html

Rahman, F. (2007a). Shia Islam. *Encarta Encyclopedia*. Retrieved April 28, 2008 from http://encarta.msn.com/encyclopedia_761570168/Shia_Islam.html

Rahman, F. (2007b). Sunni Islam. *Encarta*. Retrieved April 28, 2008 from http://encarta.msn.com/encyclopedia_761565794/sunni_islam.html

Rajhans, G. (2013, August 9). The Hindu concept of Heaven and Hell. *Speaking Tree*. Retrieved from https://www.speakingtree.in/blog/the-hindu-concept-of-heaven-and-hell

Ramakrishna, S. (n.d.). Hinduism: Ethics and business. *EENI School of International Business*. Retrieved May 16,

2019 from http://en.reingex.com/Hinduism-Business.shtml

Rao, P. (2015). HRM trends in India: A professional perspective. *Strategic HR Review, 14(1/2)*. Retrieved from https://doi.org/10.1108/SHR-01-2015-0002

Reincarnation. (2018). In *Encyclopedia Britannica*. Retrieved May 16, 2019 from https://www.britannica.com/topic/reincarnation

Religious congregations and membership study, 2000. (n.d.). *The Association of Religion Data Archives*. Retrieved May 27, 2019 from http://www.thearda.com/Archive/Files/Descriptions/RCMSST.asp

Religious membership in the United States. (2008). In *World Almanac for Kids*. Retrieved April 24, 2008 from http://www.worldalmanacforkids.com/WAKI-ViewArticle.aspx?pin=wak-025002&article_id=515&chapter_id=11&chapter_title=Religion&article_title=Religious_Membership_in_the_United_States

Sacks, J. (2010). *Genesis: The book of beginnings*. Amazon Digital Services.

Saleem, M. (2006). Islamic banking—a $300 billion deception. Philadelphia: Xlibris.

Sandip B. (2016, February 2). What Hinduism can teach us about business. *LinkedIn*. Retrieved from https://www.linkedin.com/pulse/what-hinduism-can-teach-us-about-business

Saxena, A. (2018). Islamic finance issues probed. *Gulf Daily News Online*. Retrieved from http://www.gdnonline.com/Details/443487

Schumacher, E.F. (1973). *Small is beautiful: Economics as if people mattered*. New York: Harper

Sethi, S.P., & Steidlmeier, P. (2015, January 21). Hinduism and business ethics. *Wiley Online Library*. Retrieved from https://onlinelibrary.wiley.com/doi/abs/10.1002/978 1118785317.weom020119

Seveners. (2018). In *Encyclopedia Britannica*. Retrieved May 10, 2018 from https://www.britannica.com/topic/Seveners

Shaivism. (2016, October 29). *ReligionFacts*. Retrieved from http://www.religionfacts.com/shaivism

Shaktism. (n.d.). The heart of Hinduism. Retrieved May 16, 2019 from https://iskconeducationalservices.org/HoH/tradition /1203.htm

Sharbatly, A. (2016). Risk regulation in Islamic banking: Does Saudi Arabia need to adopt the risk regulation practices of Basel? Doctoral Dissertation. University of Westminster. Retrieved from https://westminsterresearch.westminster.ac.uk/item/ 9zyvq/risk-regulation-in-islamic-banking-does-saudi-arabia-need-to-adopt-the-risk-regulation-practices-of-basel

Singh, R.K., & Sharma, P. (2013, September 4). India lacks business ethics. *The Hindu Business Line*. Retrieved from https://www.thehindubusinessline.com/opinion/Indi a-lacks-business-ethics/article20655619.ece

Smarta tradition. (n.d.). In *Wikipedia*. Retrieved May 16, 2019 from https://en.wikipedia.org/wiki/Smarta_tradition

Srivastava, S. (2018, October 11). Company and business law in India – All you need to know. *MyAdvo*. Retrieved from https://www.myadvo.in/blog/company-and-business-law-in-india/

Sujato (2010, April 15). Buddhist numerology. *Sujato Blog*. Retrieved from https://sujato.wordpress.com/2010/04/15/Buddhist-numerology

Suzuki, Y. (2016). Shariah minds in Islamic finance / Mohd David Bakar. Retrieved from https://www.researchgate.net/publication/316712577 _Shariah_Minds_in_Islamic-Finance_Mohd_Daud_Bakar

Synagogue services. (n.d.). *Israel & Judaism Studies*. Retrieved May 16, 2019 from http://www.ijs.org.au/Synagogue-services/default.aspx

Tabory, E. (1983). Reform and Conservative Judaism in Israel: A social and religious profile. *American Jewish*

Year Book. Retrieved from
https://www.jstor.org/stable/23604806?seq=1#page_s
can_tab_contents

Taxes. (2018). Income tax slabs. *Insurance Knowledge Centre.* Retrieved from
https://www.hdfclife.com/insurance-knowledge-centre/tax-saving-insurance/latest-income-tax-slab-and-deductions-fy-2017-18

Ten Buddhist Maxims for Business. (n.d.). *Business Insurance Quotes.* Retrieved May 17, 2019 from
http://www.businessinsurance.org/10-buddhist-maxims-for-business/

Thakur, N. (2007). How to set sukuk free. *International Financial Law Review, 16*(12), 20. Retrieved from
https://www.iflr.com/Article/1976852/How-to-set-sukuk-free.html?ArticleId=1976852

The Israeli courts and legal system: A brief synopsis. (2014, October 25). *United with Israel.* Retrieved from
https://unitedwithisrael.org/the-israeli-courts-and-legal-system-a-brief-synopsis/

The major systems and their literature. (n.d.). In *Encyclopedia Britannica.* Retrieved May 16, 2019 from
https://www.britannica.com/topic/Buddhism/The major-systems-and-their-literature

The Torah: Five books of story, law, and poetry divided into 54 weekly portions. (n.d.). *My Jewish Learning.* Retrieved from https://www.myjewishlearning.com/article/the-torah/

Timeline for the history of Judaism. (n.d.). *Jewish Virtual Library*. Retrieved May 15, 2019 from http://www.jewishvirtuallibrary.org/timeline-for-the-history-of-judaism

Timeline of Buddhist history. (n.d.). *Buddha Dharma Education Association & BuddhaNet*. Retrieved May 17, 2019 from https://www.buddhanet.net/e-learning/history/b_chron-txt.htm

Tole, J.T. (2012). Israel's high power/low power & high/low uncertainty avoidance. Retrieved from https://jarretttole.wordpress.com/2012/10/09/israels-high-powerlow-power-highlow-uncertainity-avoidance/

Trammell, S. (2005). Islamic finance. *CFA Magazine*. March-April, 16-23.

Tsuji. T. (n.d.). On reincarnation. *Buddha Dharma Education Association & BuddhaNet*. Retrieved May 17, 2019 from https://www.buddhanet.net/e-learning/reincarnation.htm

Types of dress and vestments in Eastern religions. (2018). In *Encyclopedia Britannica*. Retrieved May 16, 2019 from https://www.britannica.com/topic/religious-dress/Types-of-dress-and-vestments-in-Eastern-religions

Understanding riba in Islamic finance. (n.d.). *Azzad Asset Management*. Retrieved May 14, 2019 from https://www.azzadfunds.com/understanding-riba-in-islamic-finance/

University Islamic Financial. (n.d.). Retrieved August 27, 2010 from http://www.universityislamicfinancial.com/homefinance

Vail, L.F. (n.d.). The origins of Buddhism. *Asia Society – Center for Global Education*. Retrieved May 17, 2019 from https://asiasociety.org/education/origins-buddhism

Violatti, C. (2013, December 13). Siddhartha Gautama. In *Ancient History Encyclopedia*. Retrieved from https://www.ancient.eu/Siddhartha_Gautama/

Violatti, C. (2018, May 8). The Vedas. In *Ancient History Encyclopedia*. Retrieved from https://www.ancient.eu/TheVedas/

Vital statistics: Jewish population of the world. (n.d.). *Jewish Virtual Library*. Retrieved May 15, 2019 from http://www.jewishvirtuallibrary.org/jewish-population-of-the-world

Warde, I. (2000). *Islamic finance in the global economy*. Edinburgh, UK: Edinburgh University Press.

Wenger, E. (n.d.). The laws of stealing. *Chabad.org*. Retrieved May 16, 2019 from http://www.chabad.org/library/article_cdo/aid/383785/jewish/The-Laws-of-Stealing.htm

What is India's caste system? (2017, July 20). *BBC News.* Retrieved from https://www.BBC.com/news/world-asia-india-35650616

What is Vaishnavism? (n.d.). *International Society for Krishna Consciousness.* Retrieved May 16, 2019 from http://www.iskcon.org/what-is-vaishnavism/

White, B. (1993). A five-minute introduction. *Buddha Dharma Education Association & Buddha Net.* Retrieved from https://www.buddhanet.net/e-learning/5minbud.htm

Worship. (2005, September 27). *BBC.* Retrieved from http://www.BBC.co.uk/religion/religions/hinduism/worship/worship.shtml

Zacharias, R. (n.d.). What is Hinduism and what do Hindus believe? *Got Questions?* Retrieved May 16, 2019 from https://www.gotquestions.org/hinduism.html

Zinser, B.A. (2015). Eterminants of United States Muslims' intentions to use retail Islamic banking and financial services: An application of the theory of planned behavior. Doctoral Dissertation. Anderson University, Anderson, IN.

This page intentionally left blank

THE AUTHORS

Samuel Dunn is a business professional who has spent his career working in education, the second largest civilian industry in the United States. He holds a PhD degree in mathematics and a DBA degree in International Business. He has travelled to over 50 countries and worked in Kenya, Brazil, and Kazakhstan. He is a futurist with multiple publications in futurism and business practices. He has served for many years as a business school accreditation commissioner. He is currently a Senior Fellow and Professor of Business at Northwest Nazarene University in Nampa, Idaho, United States.

Joshua Jensen is a seasoned business leader and leadership consultant with a longstanding career that spans many industries including higher education, K-12 education, non-profit healthcare, local government, and the private sector. He holds an EdD degree in organizational leadership as well as MBA and MPA degrees. He currently serves as the Director of Graduate Studies and Associate Professor of Leadership in the College of Business at Northwest Nazarene University in Nampa, Idaho, United States, and works to enhance the global acumen of graduate students by offering international travel experiences in conjunction with business degree programs.

Ronald Galloway has extensive experience in global business. He lived in Nicaragua for most of his youth, then came to the United States for college and graduate education. He worked in Mexico for several years in the airline industry. He holds a PhD degree in leadership and human development, an MA degree in missiology, and an MS degree in Management and Organizational Development. For many years he served as Dean of the College of Business at Northwest Nazarene University in Nampa, Idaho, United States. He previously served for many years as a business school accreditation commissioner. He has travelled to over 75 countries and worked in several foreign locations.